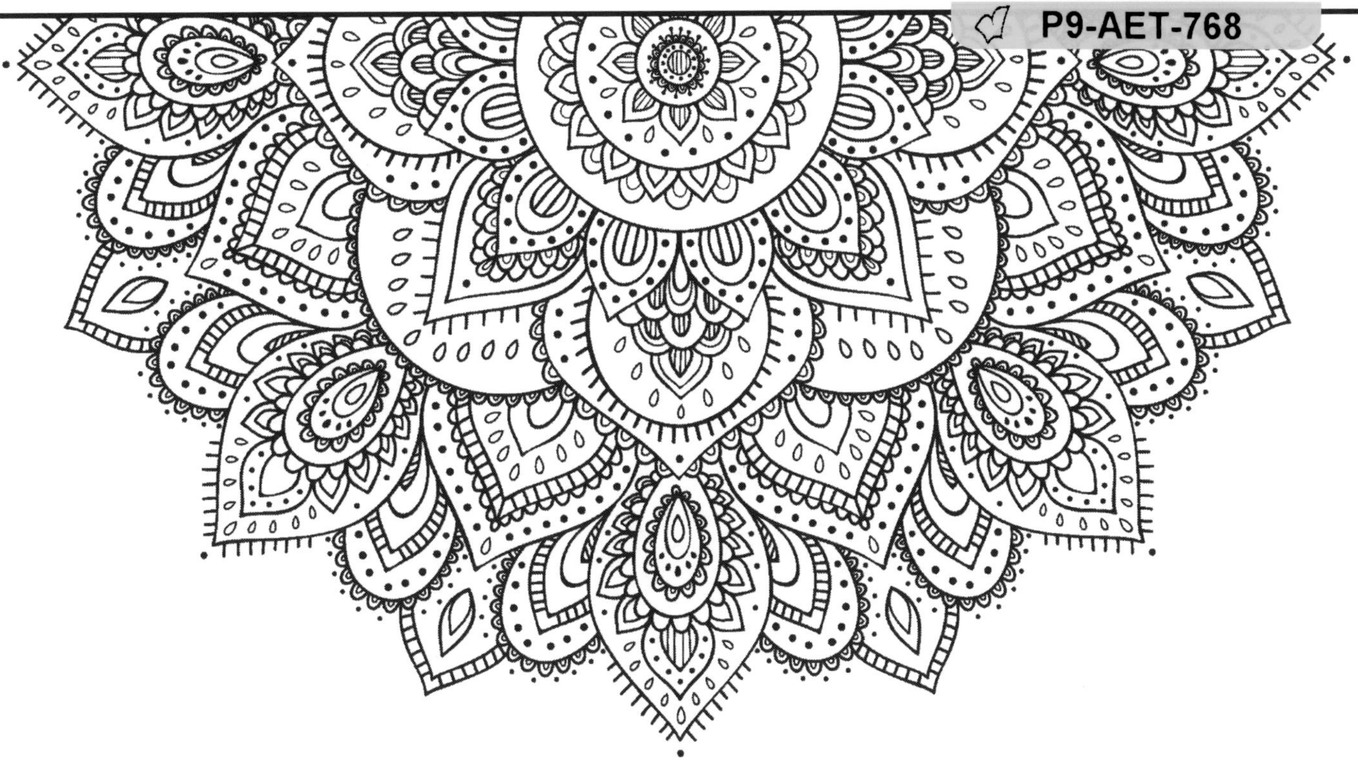

Adult Coloring Books

Zing books

Adult Coloring Books
By: Coloring Books for Adults

Follow Zing Books on Instagram @zingbooks

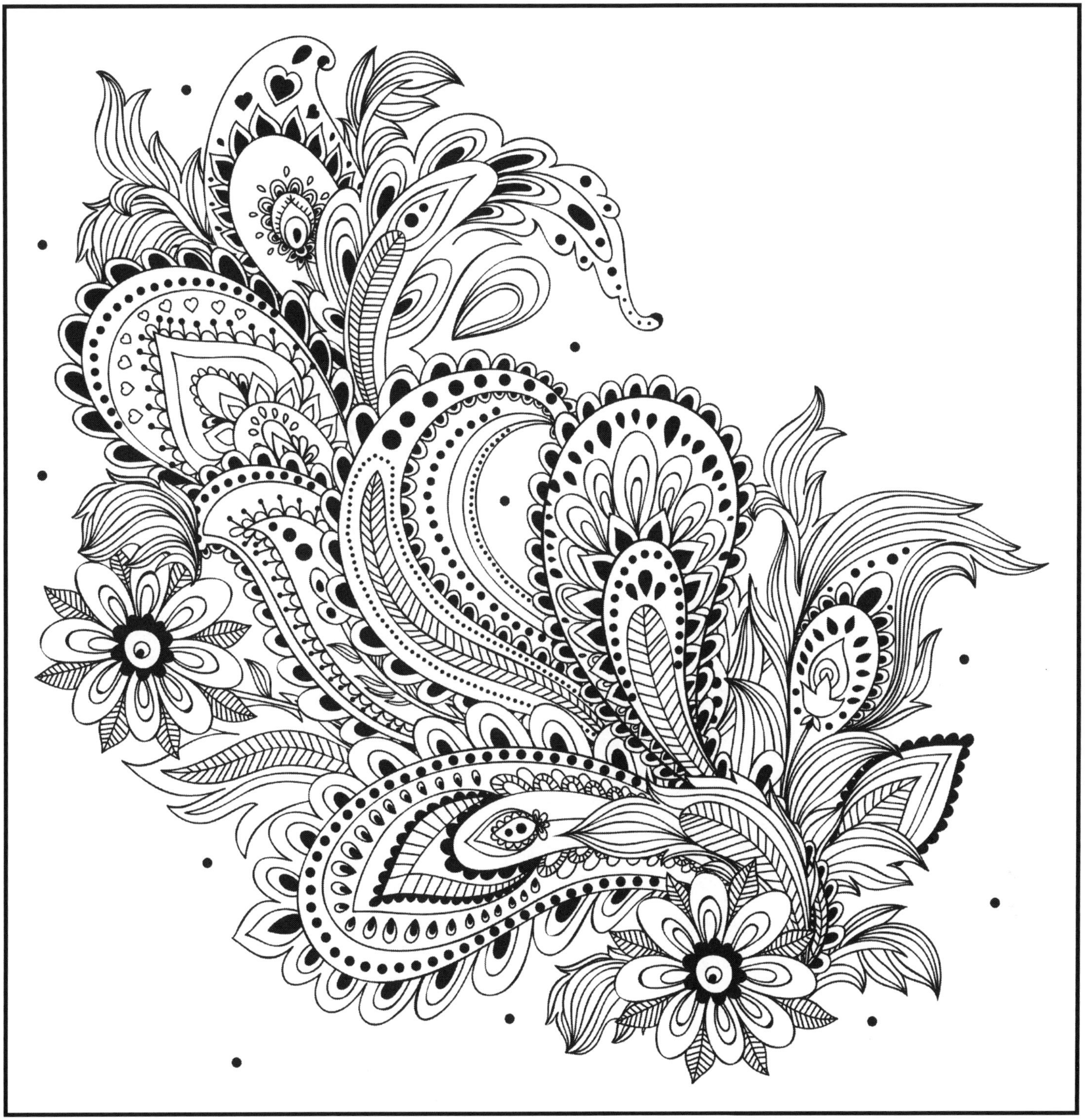

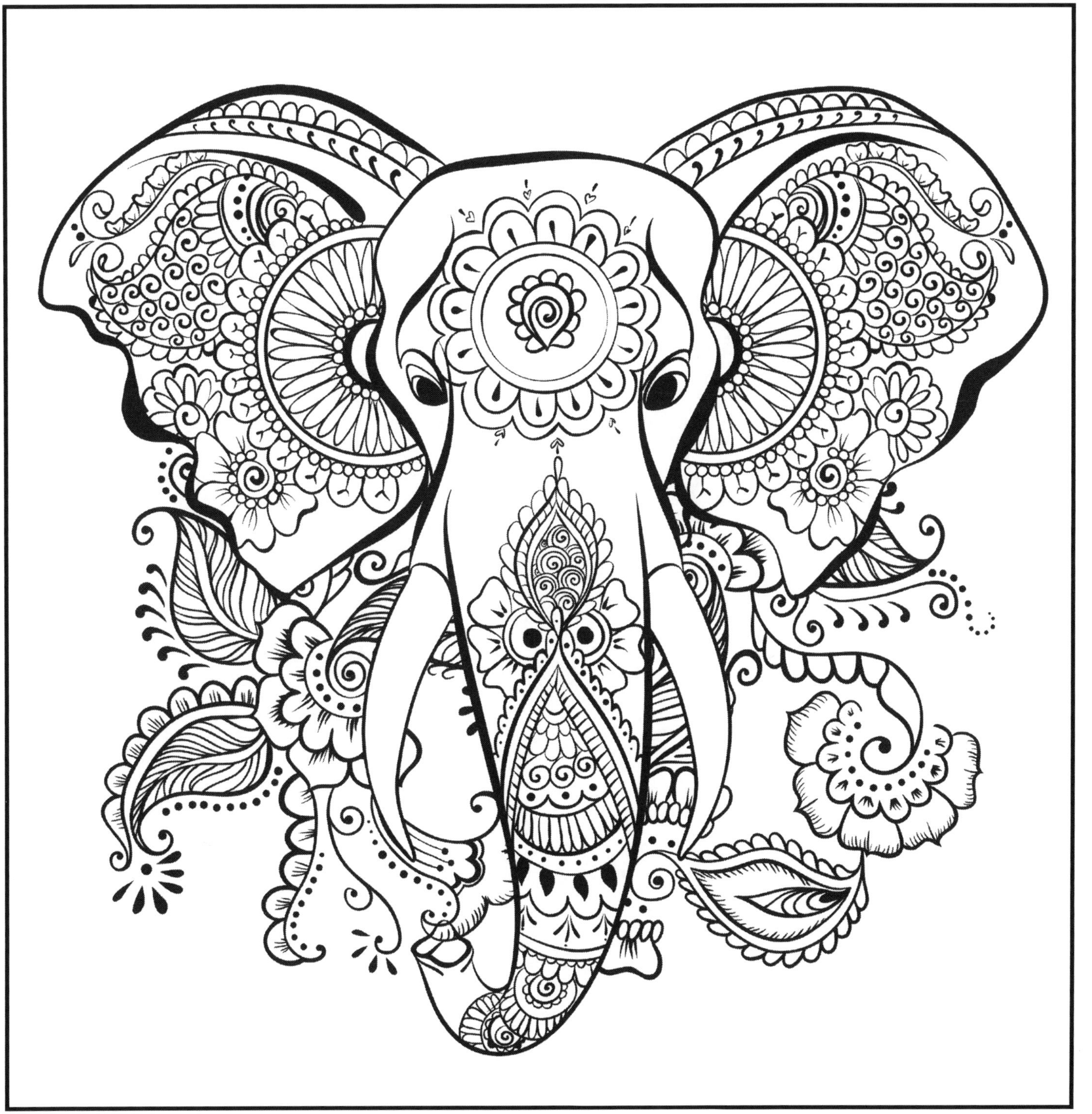

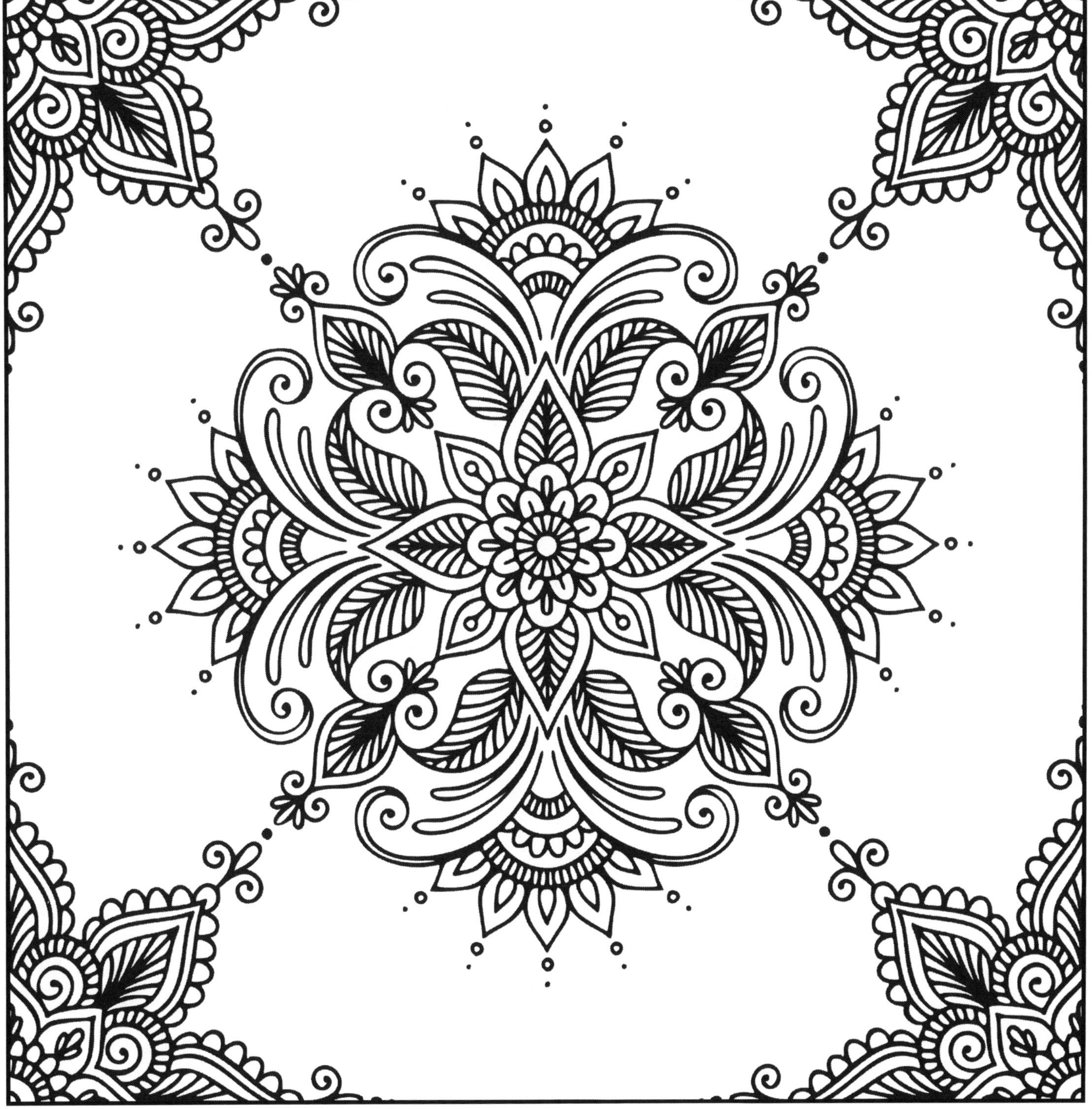

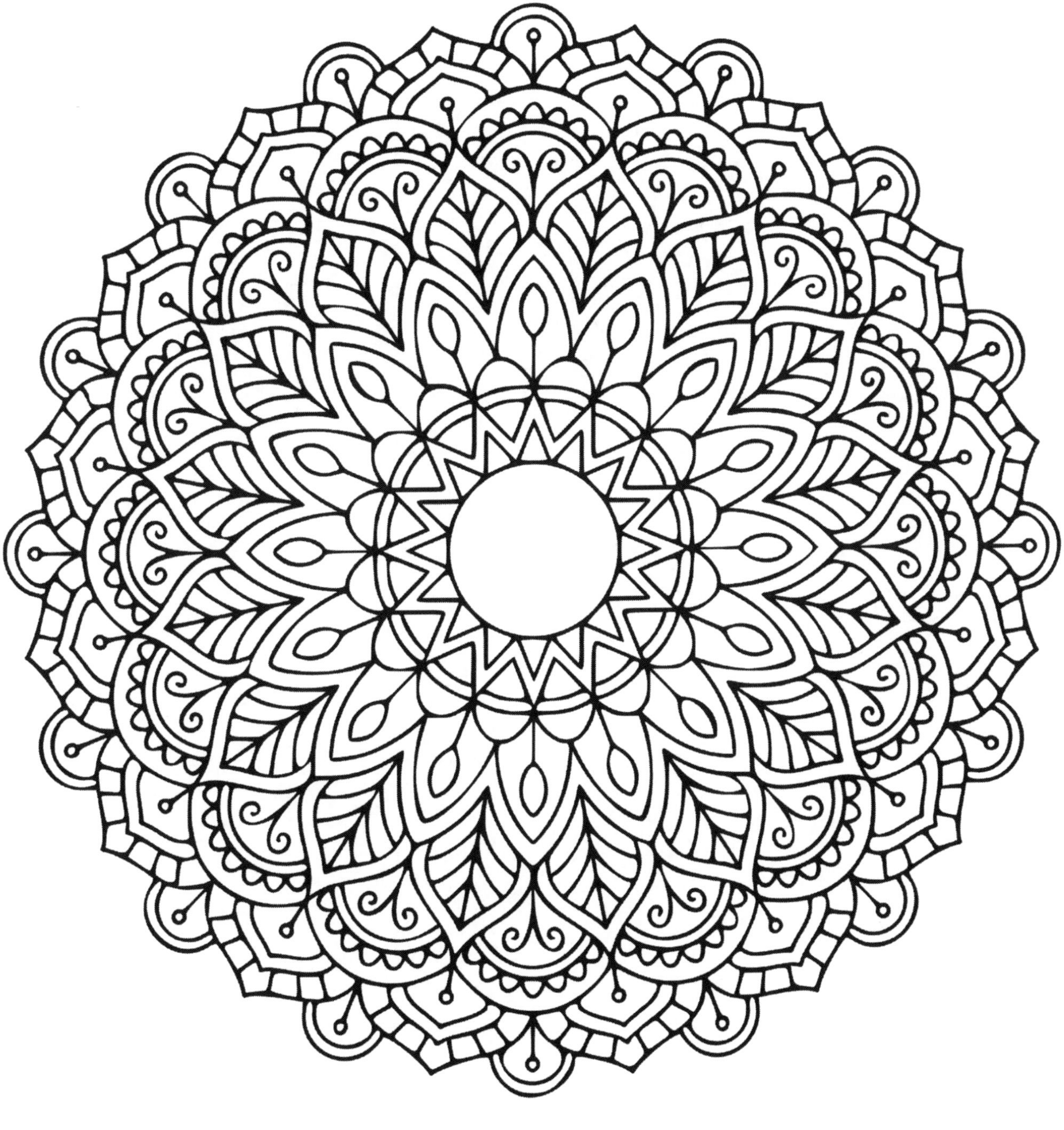

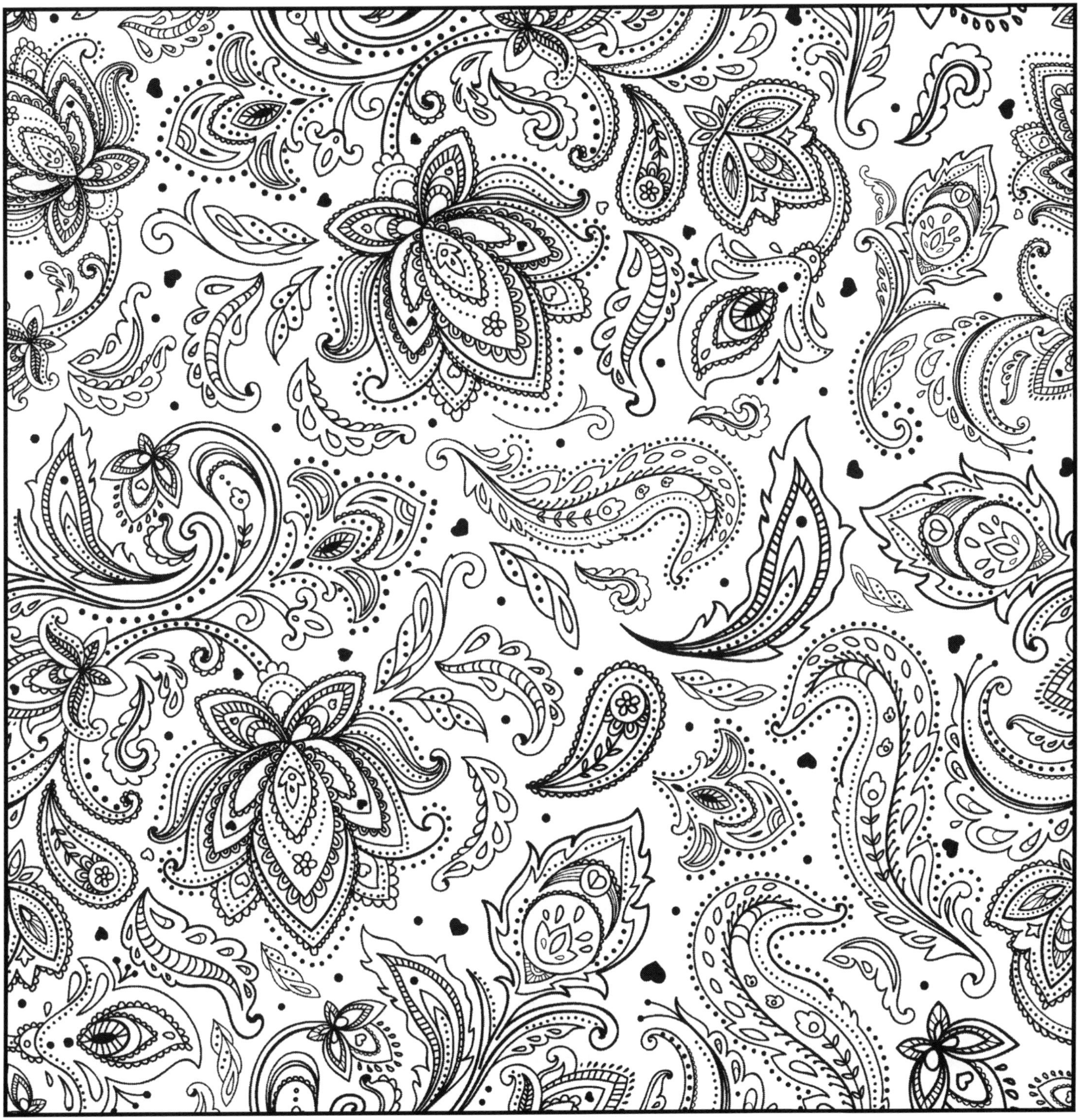

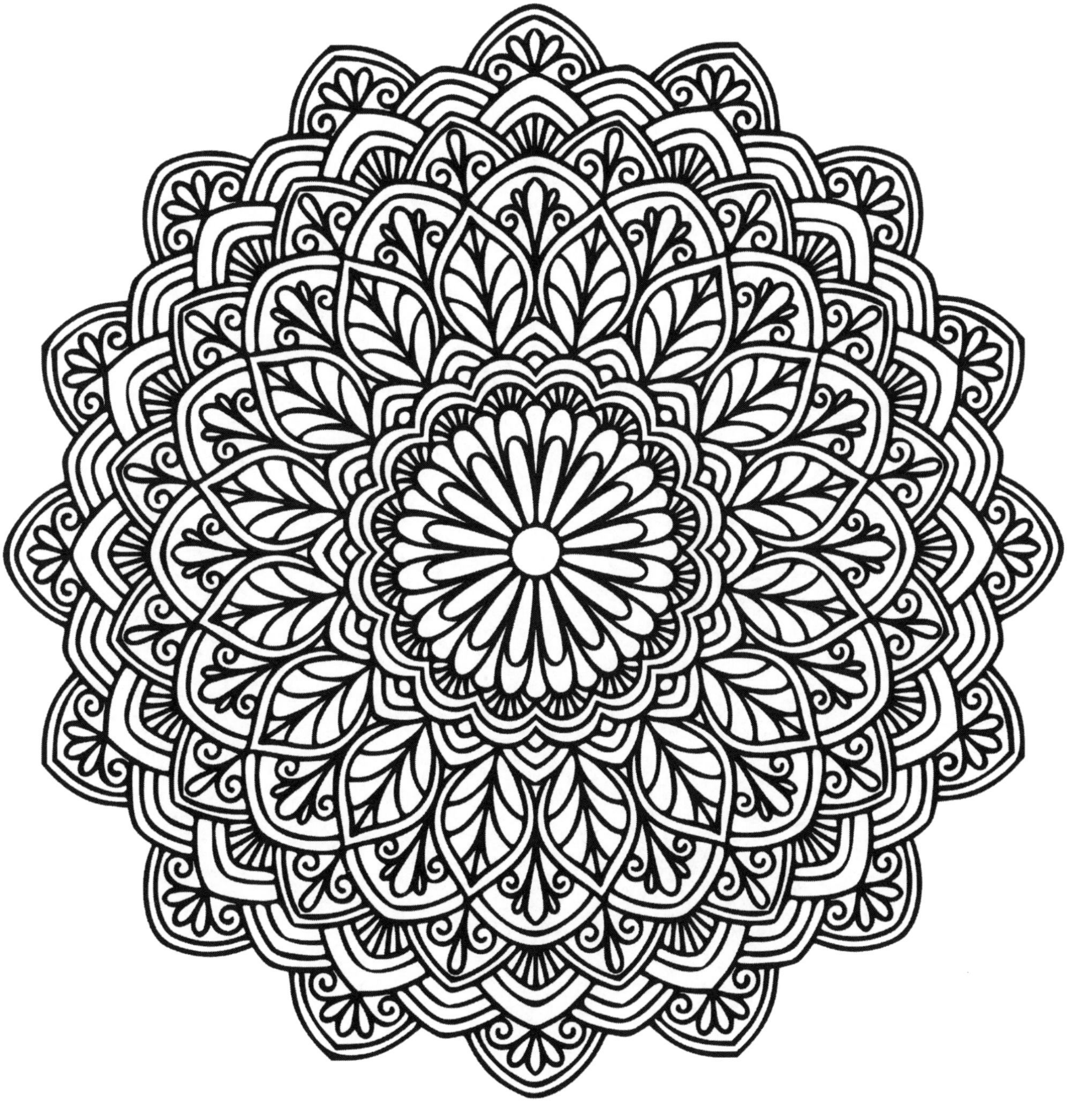

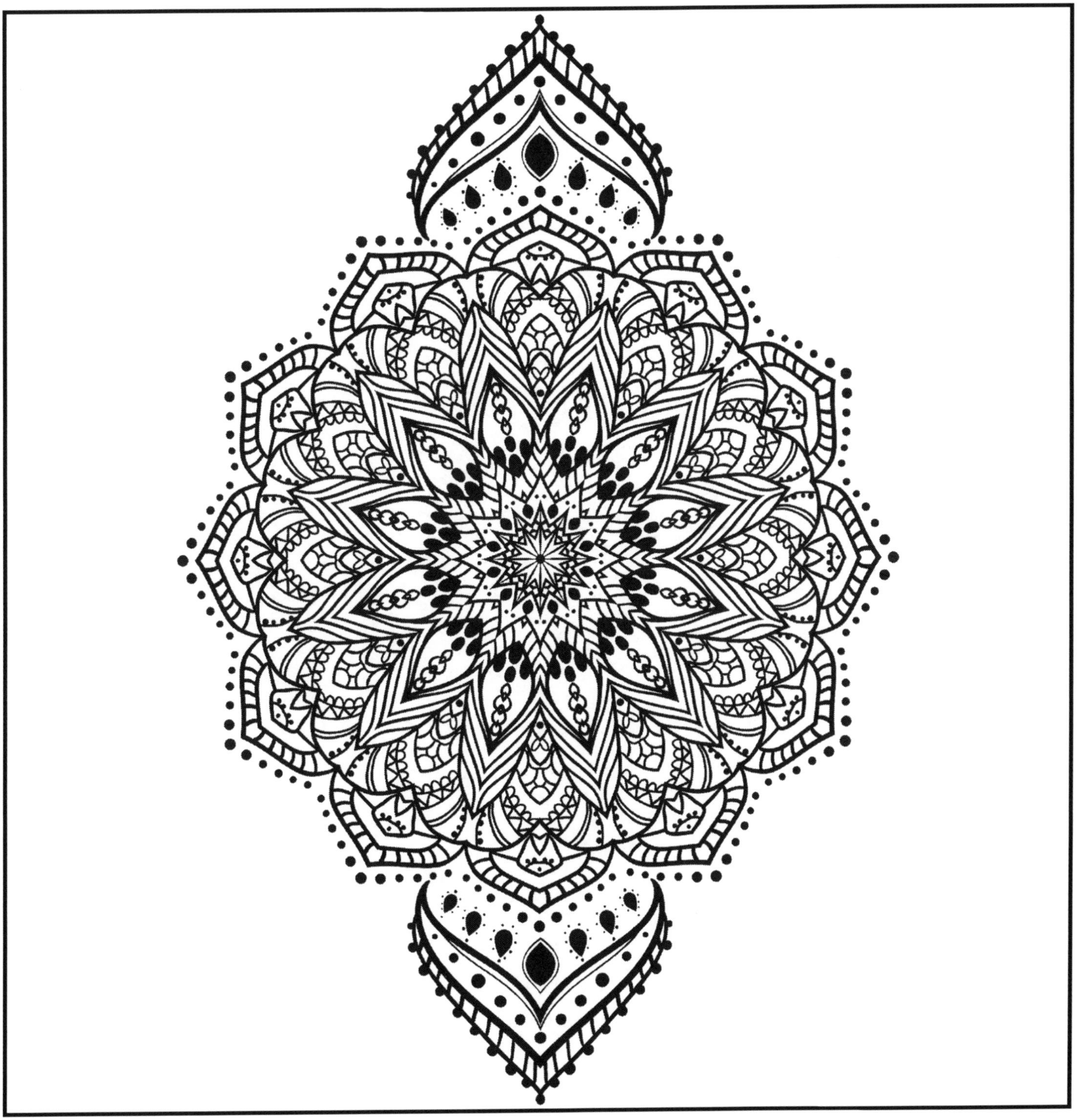

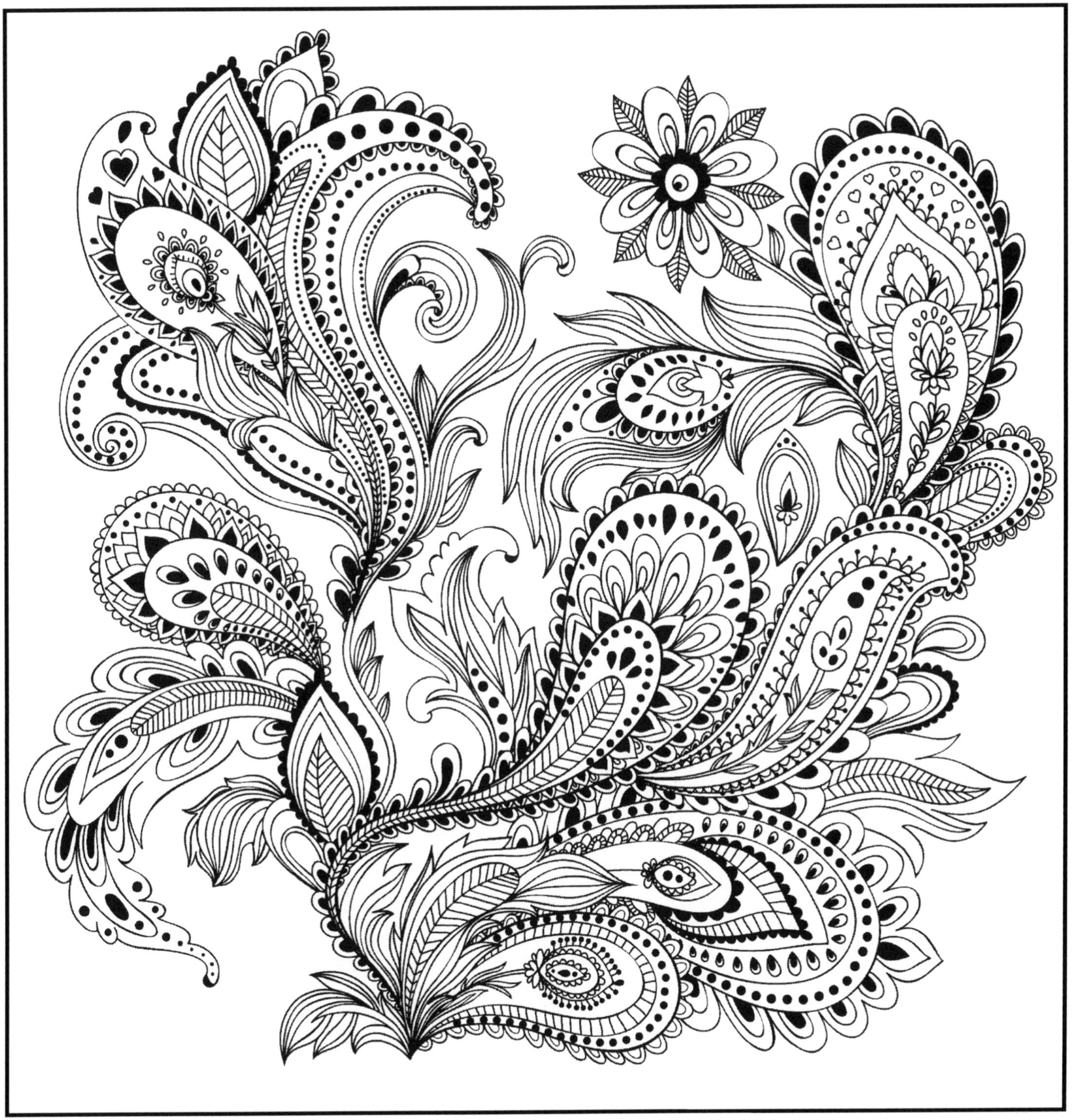

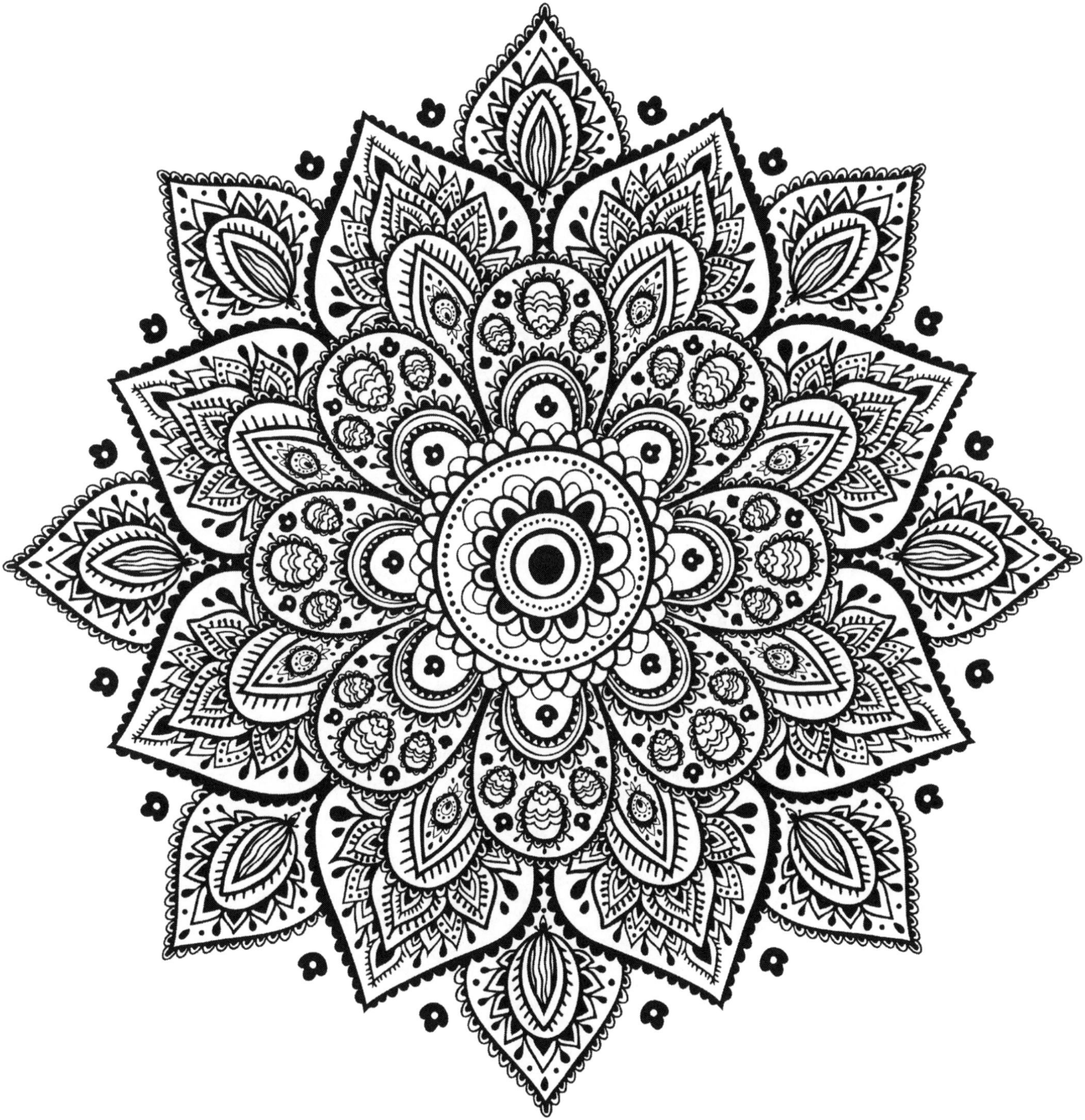

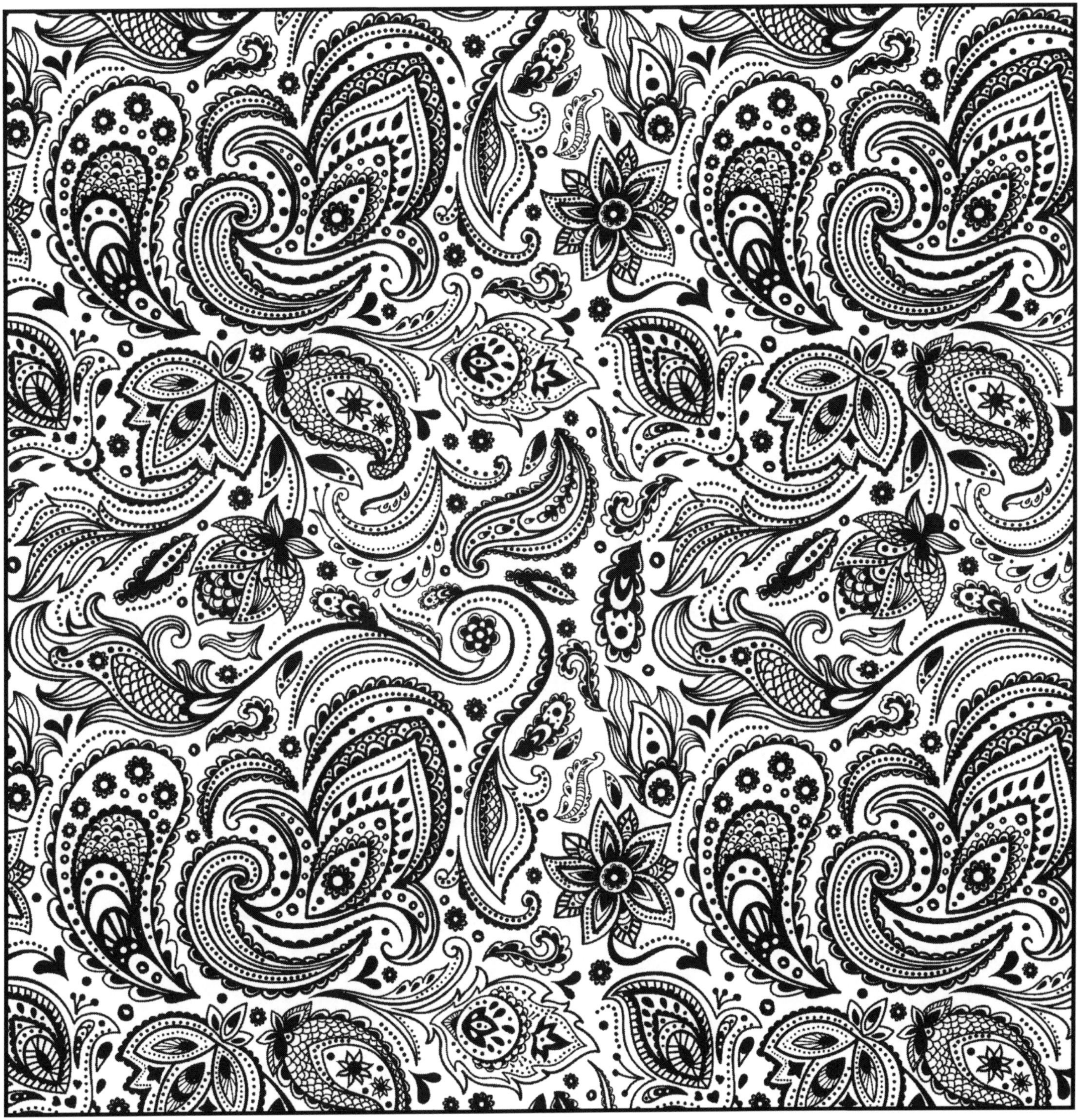

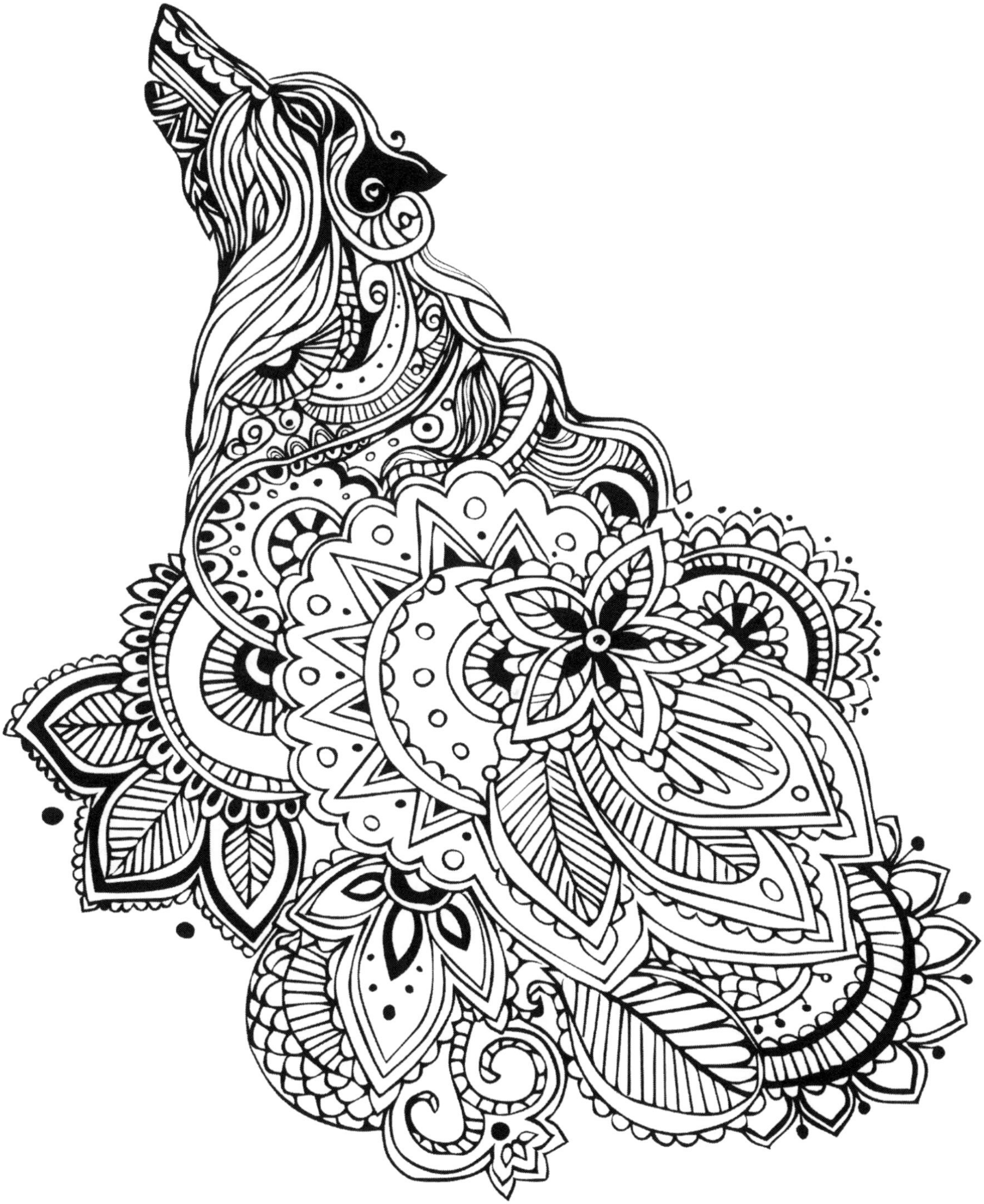

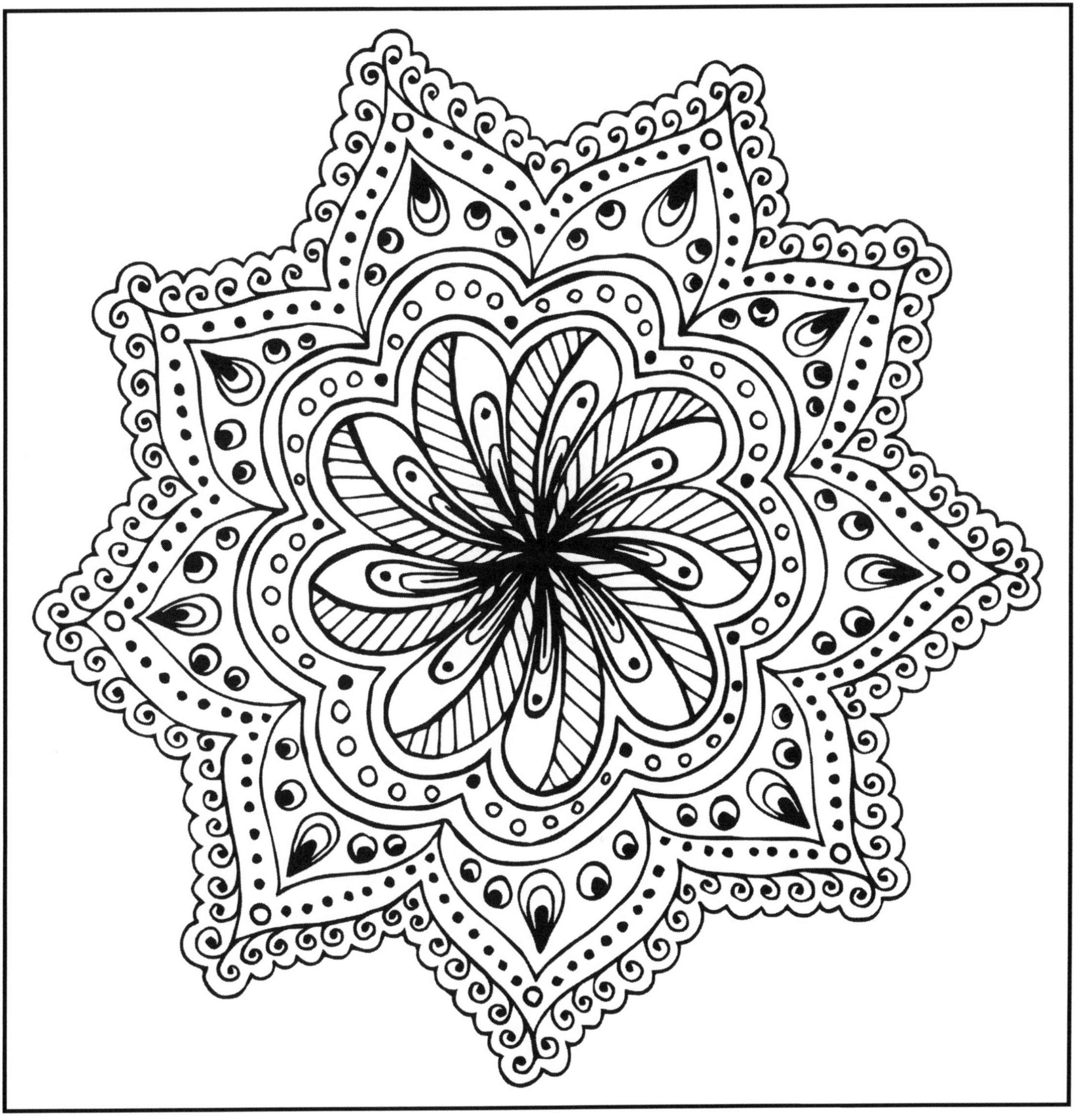

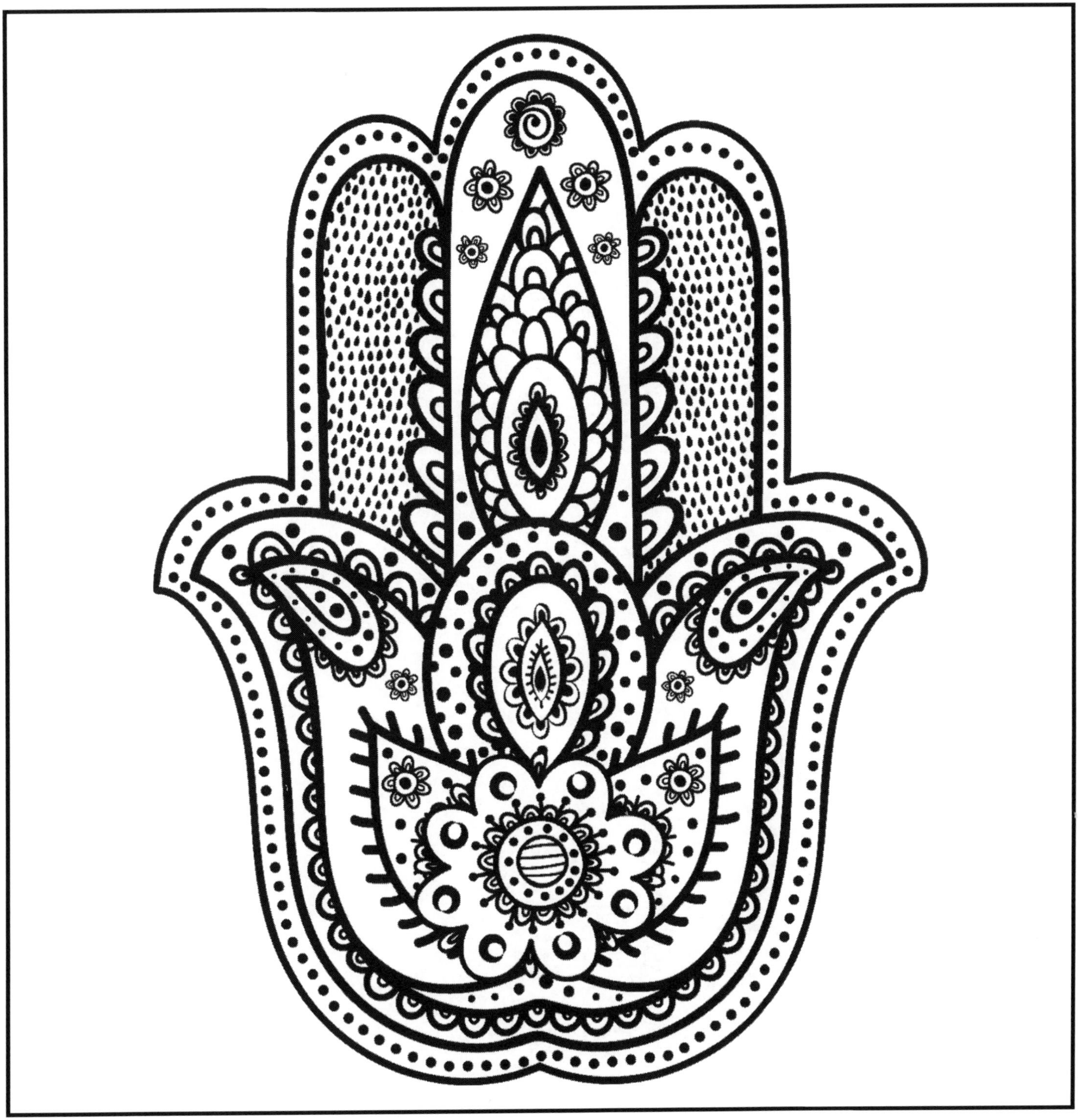

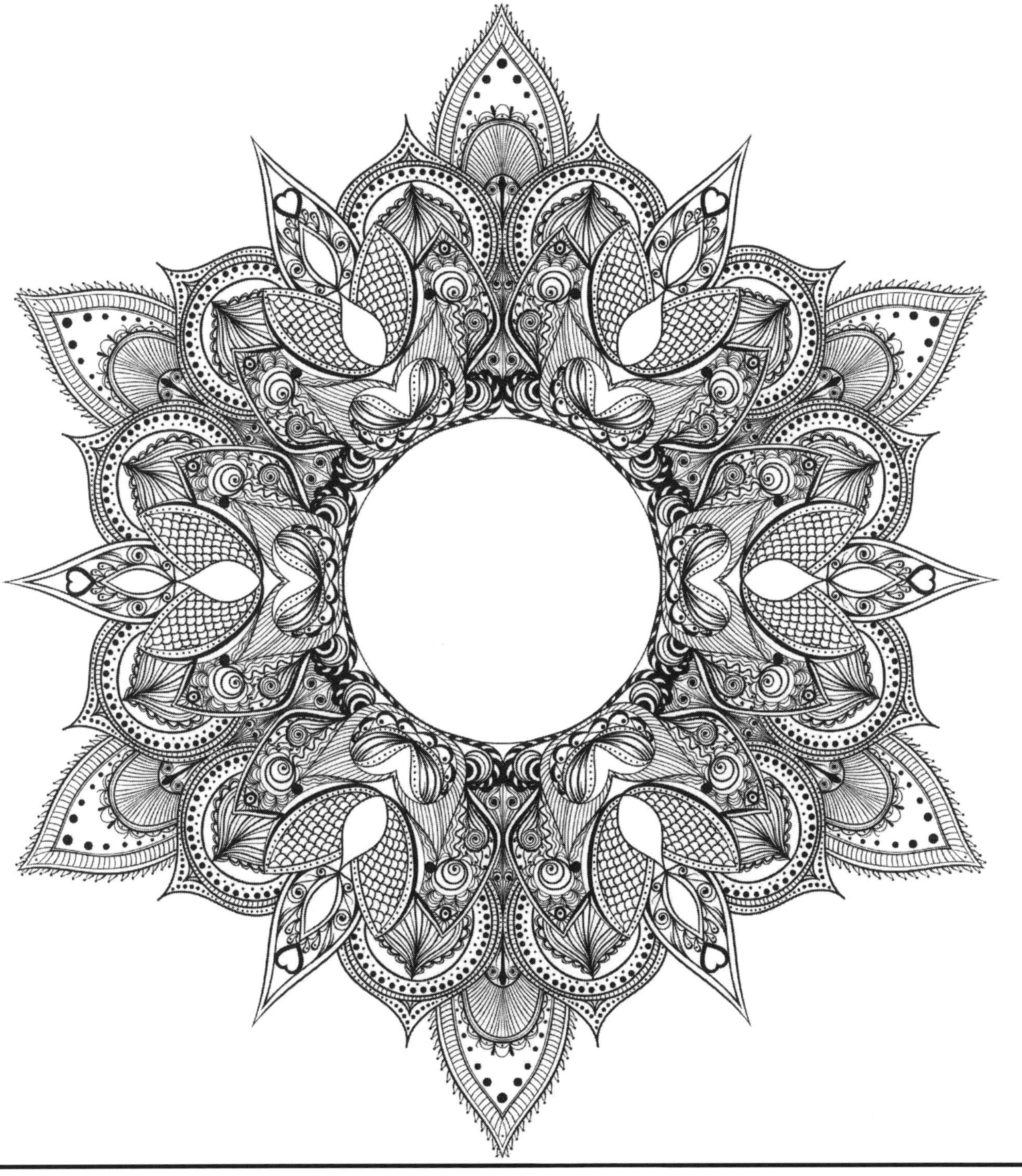

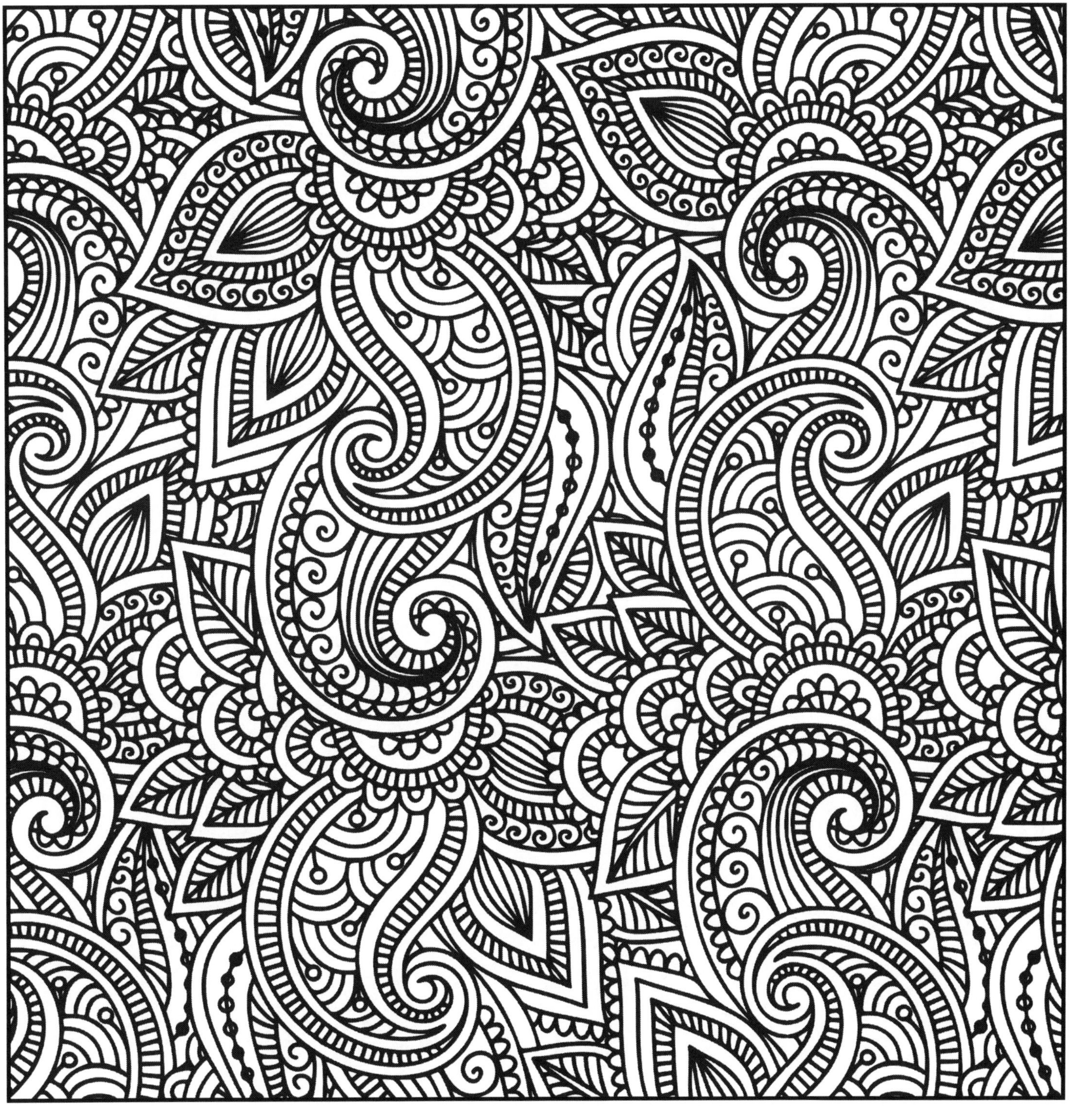

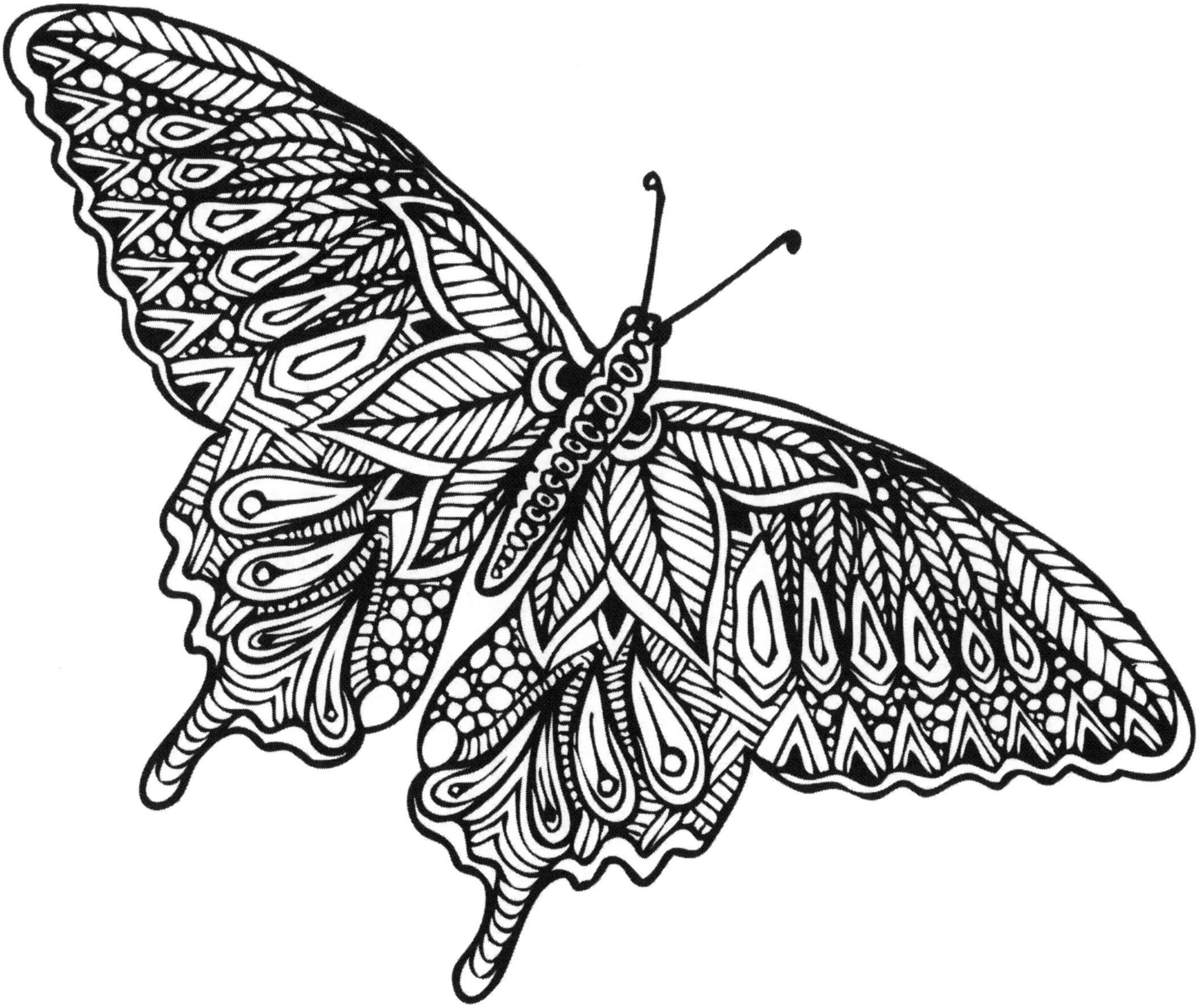

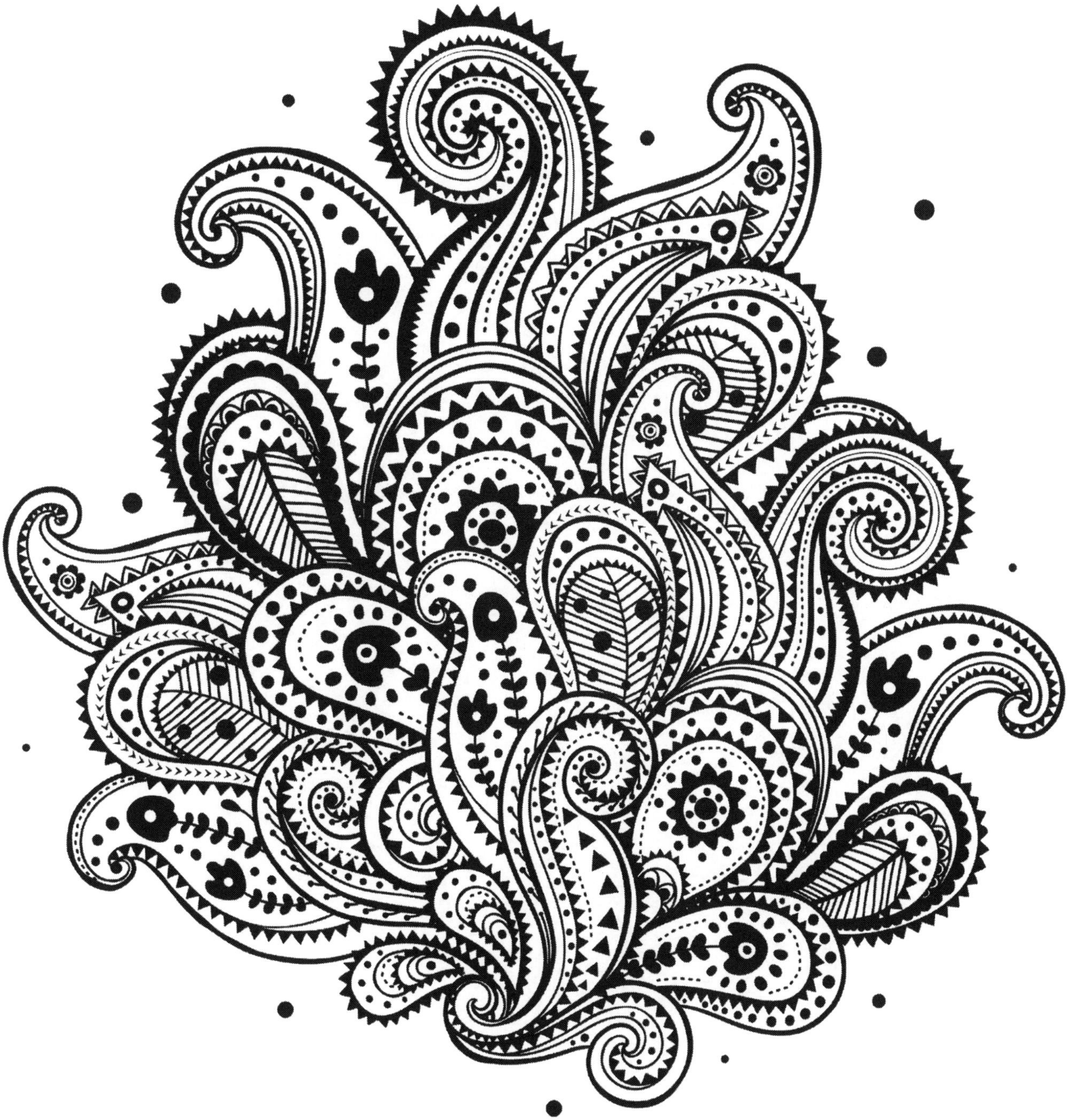

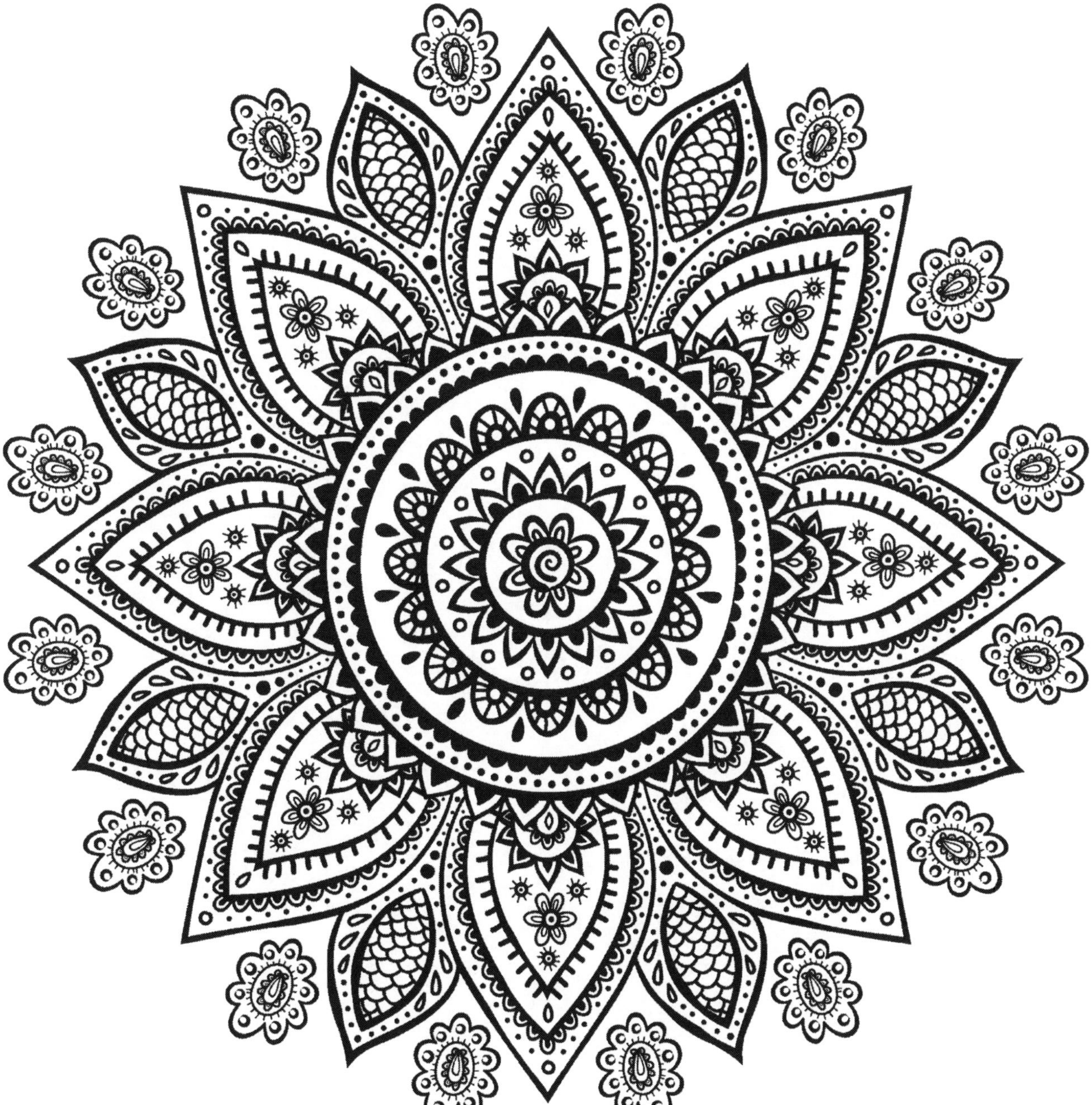

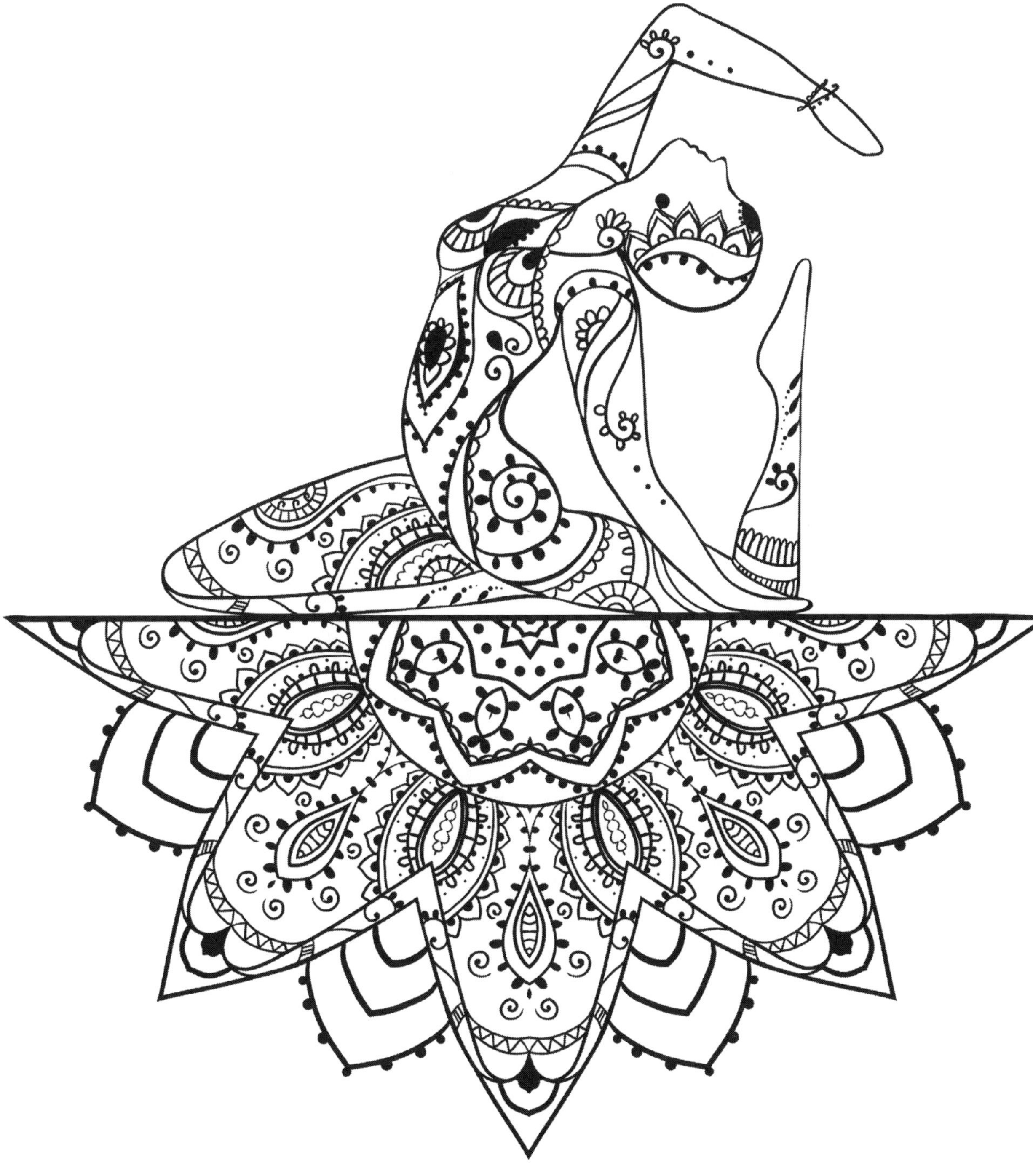

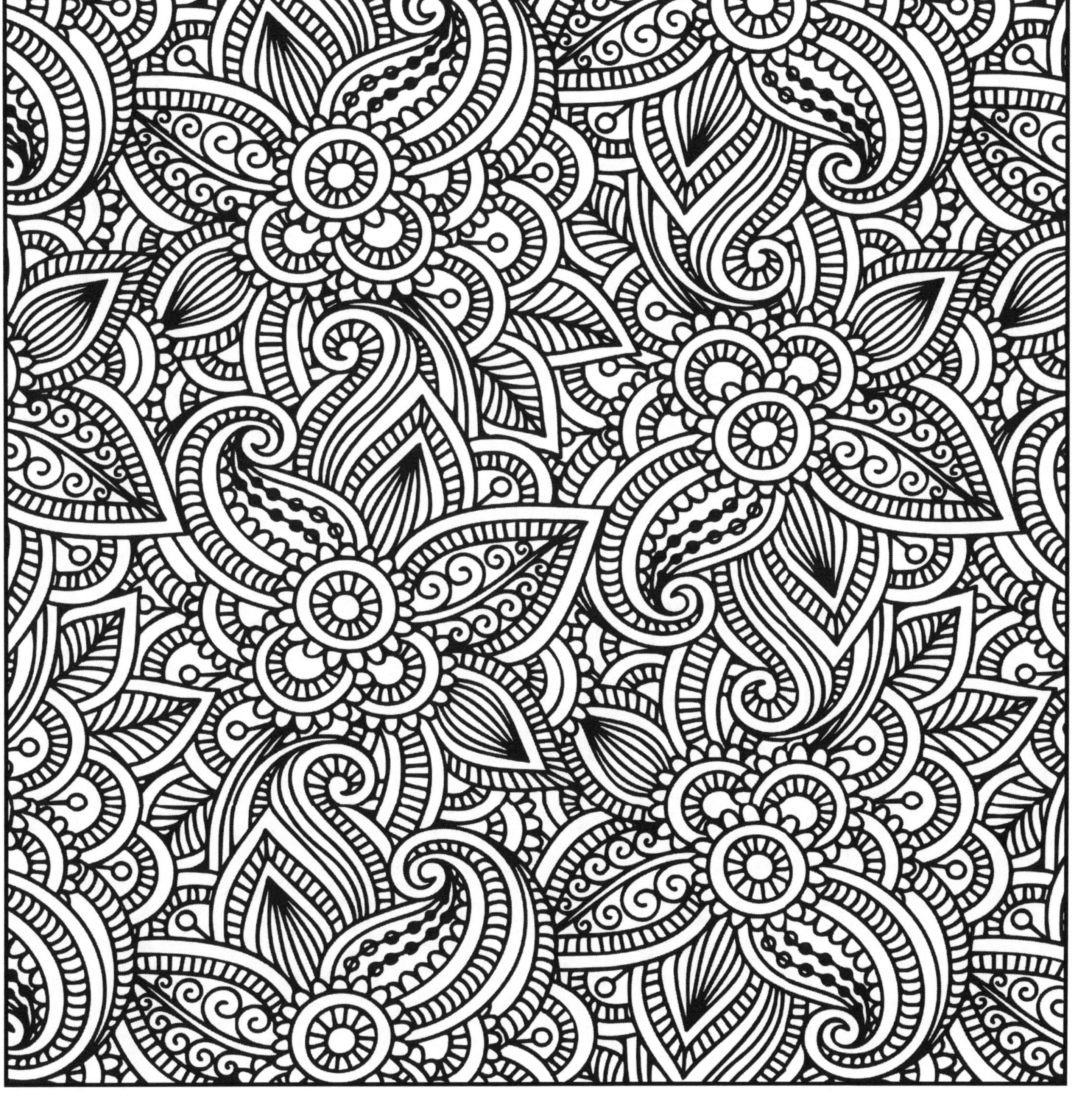

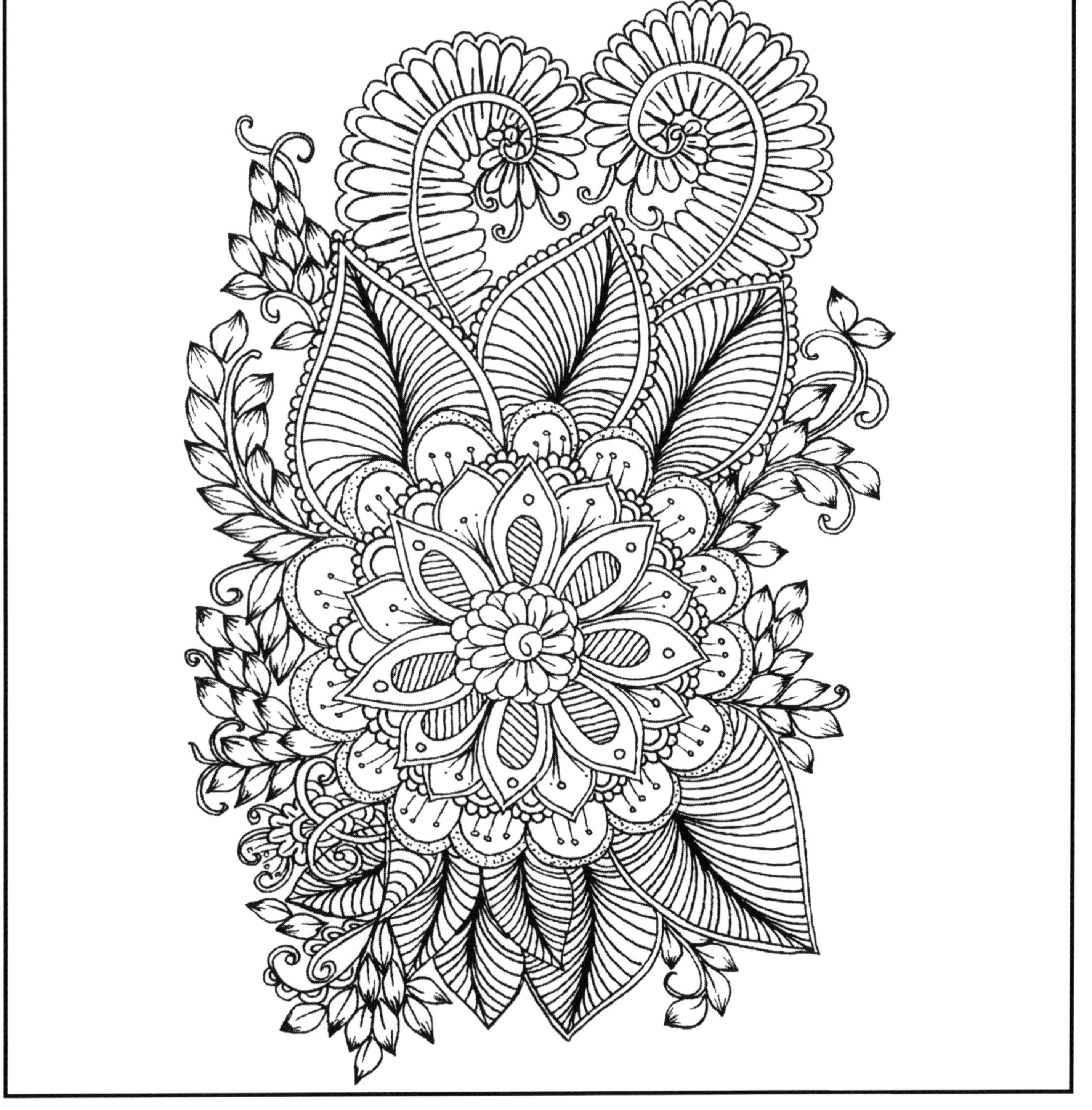

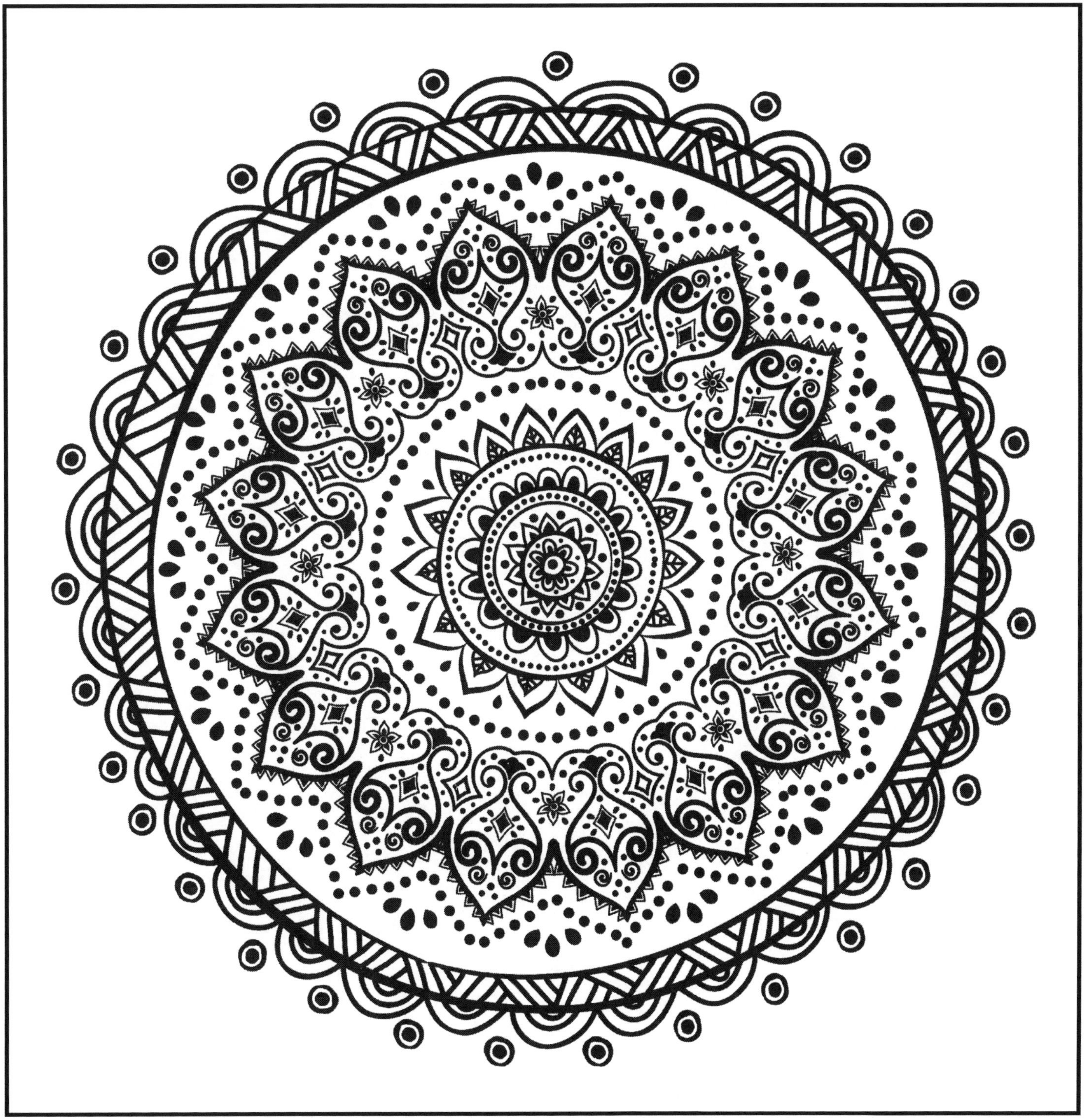

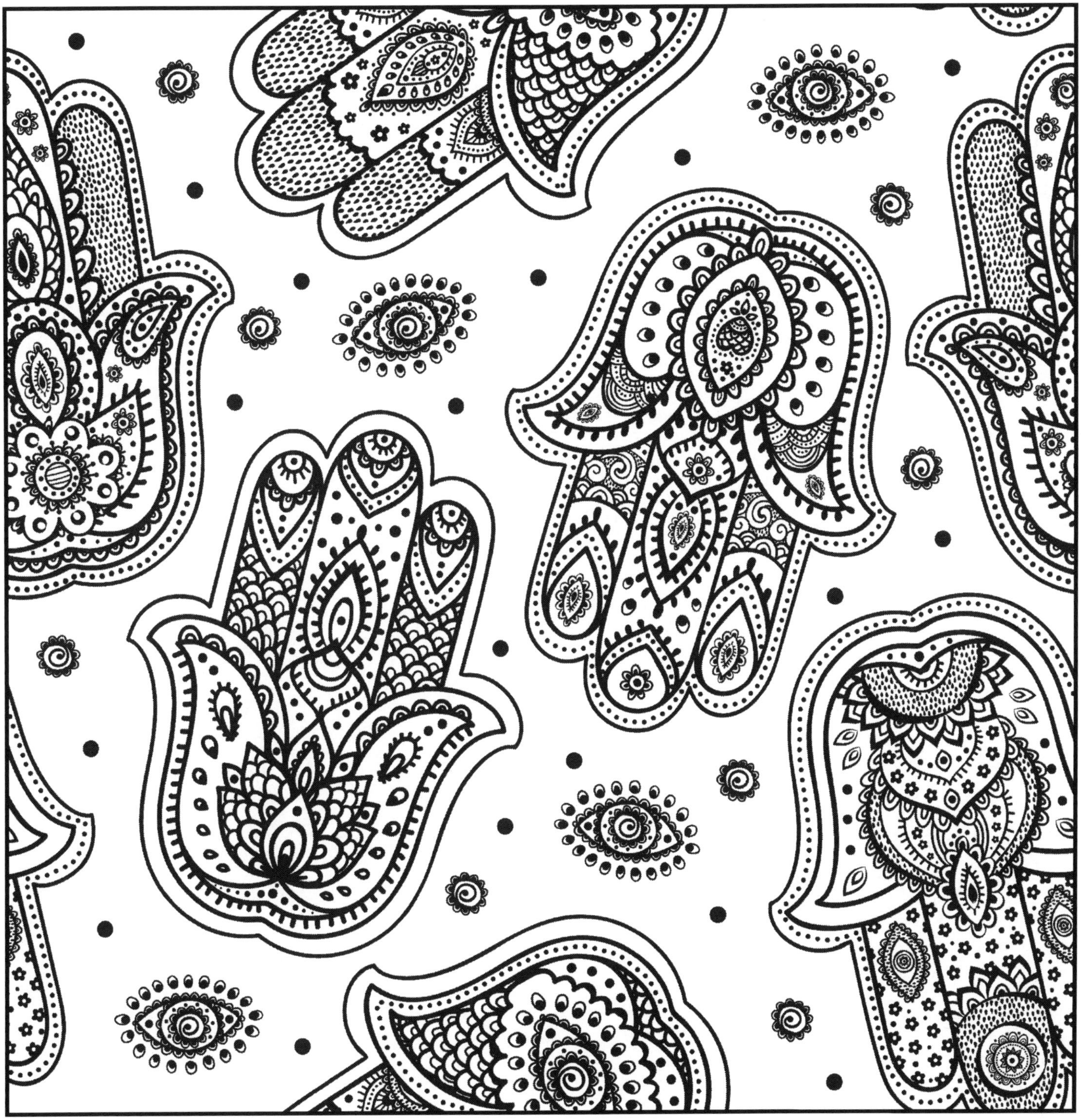

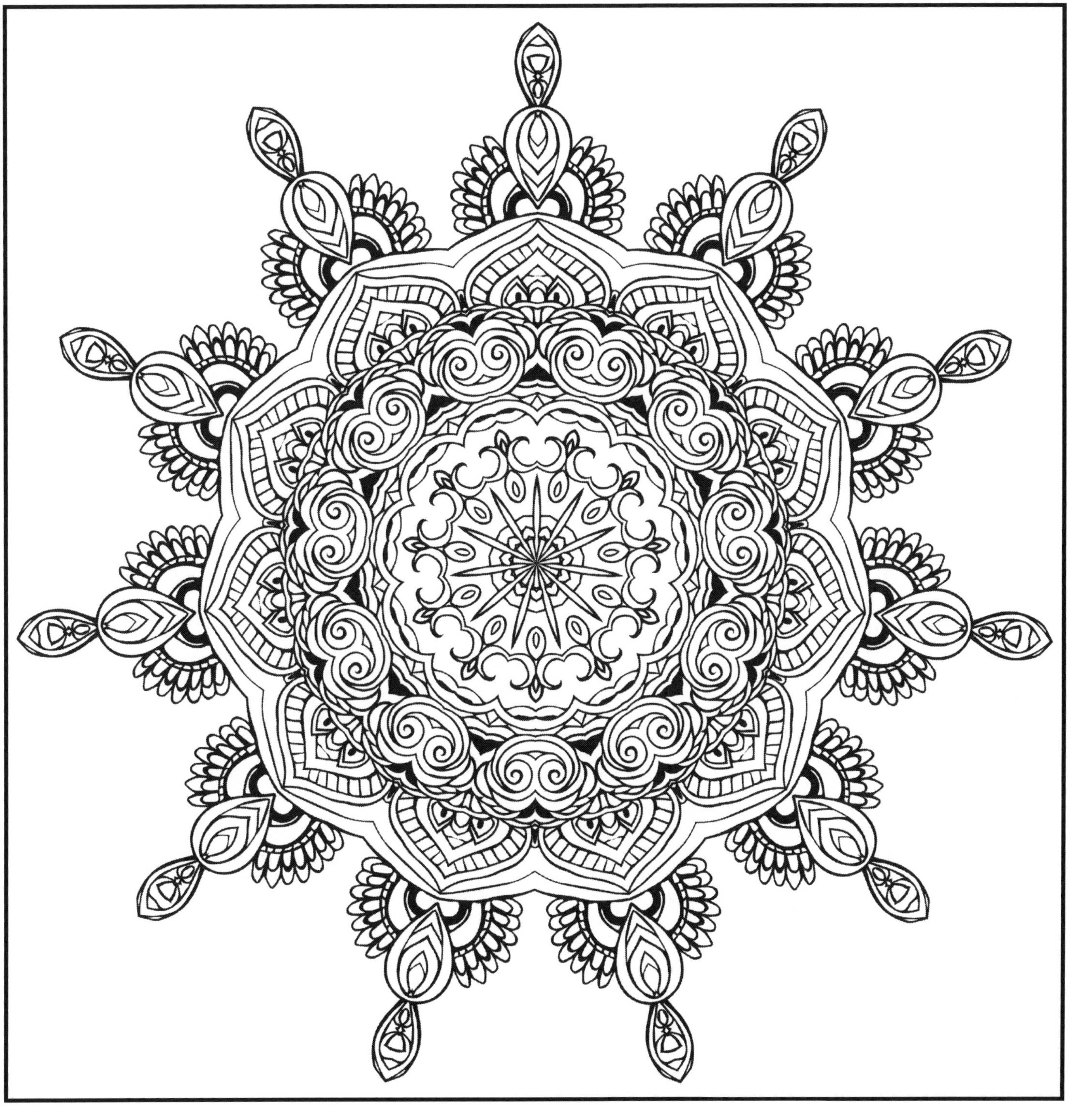

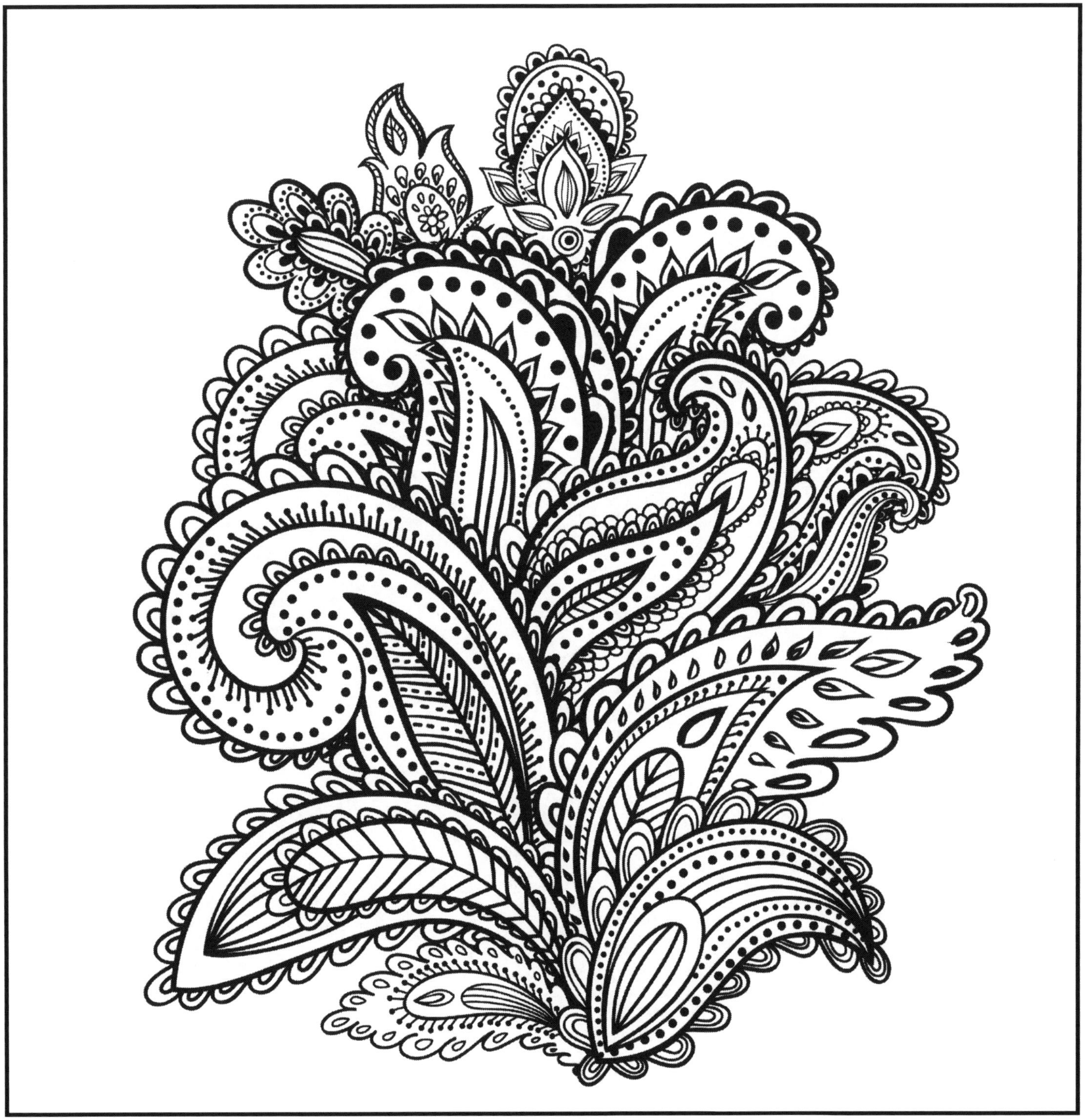

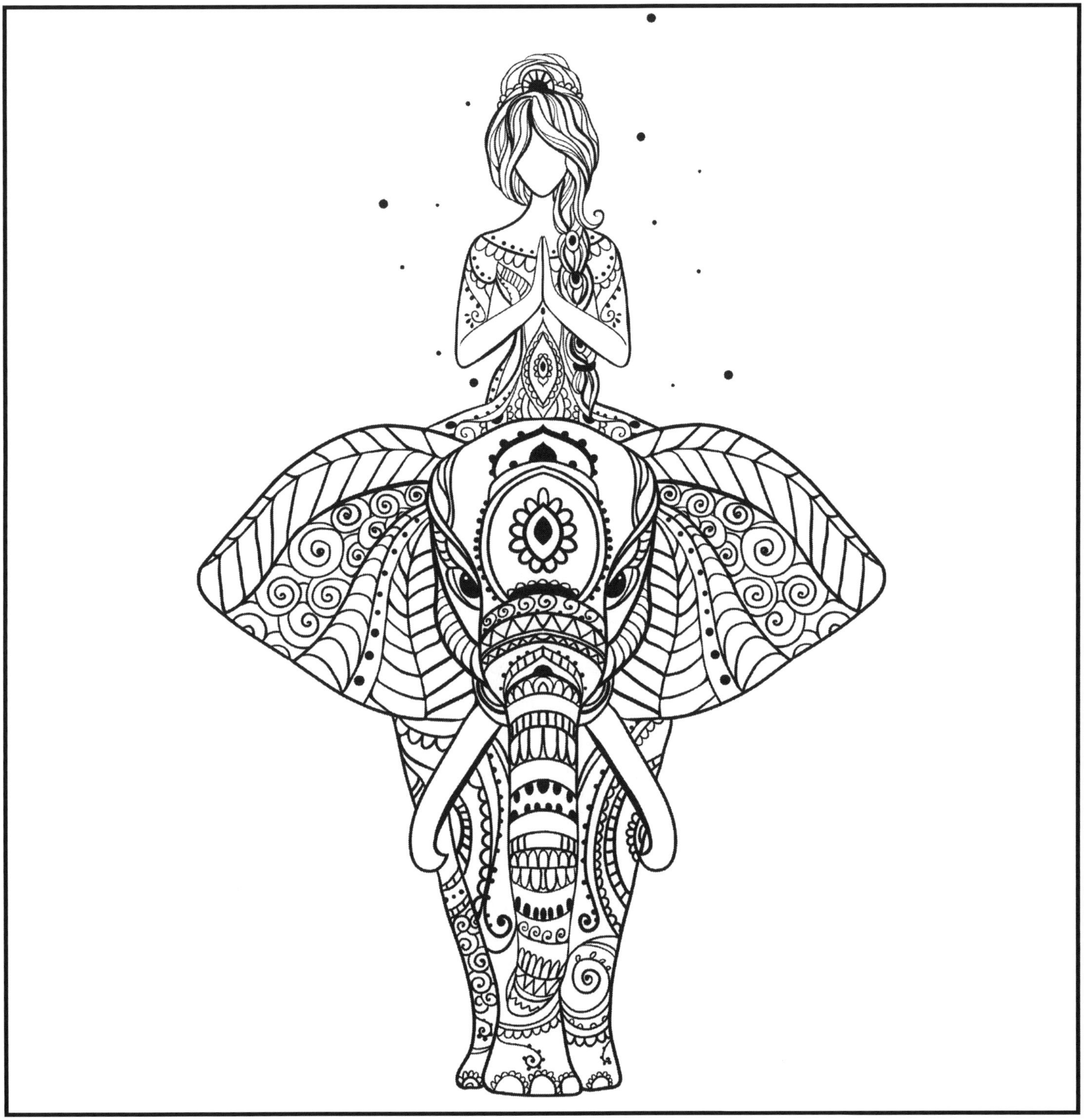

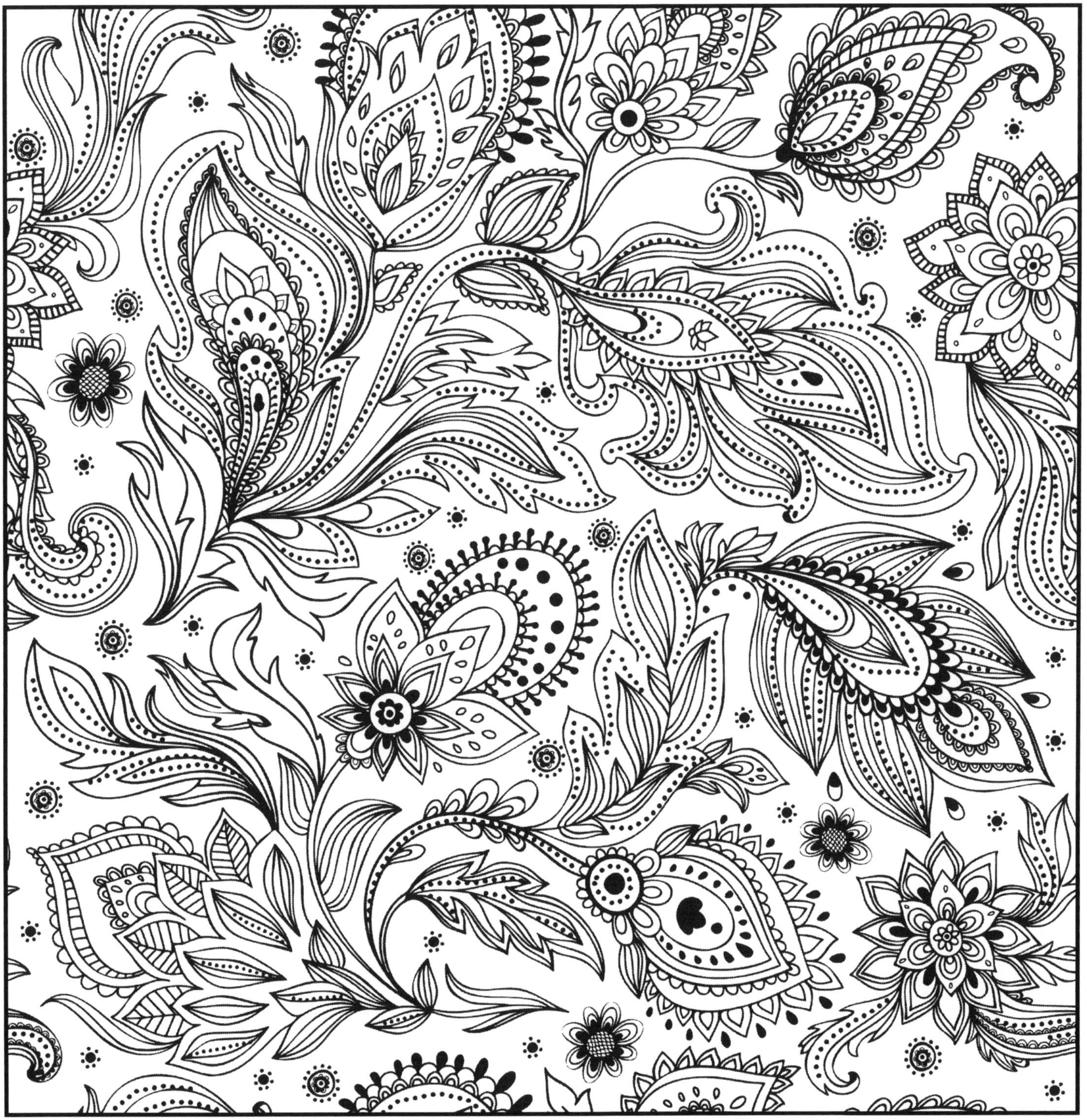

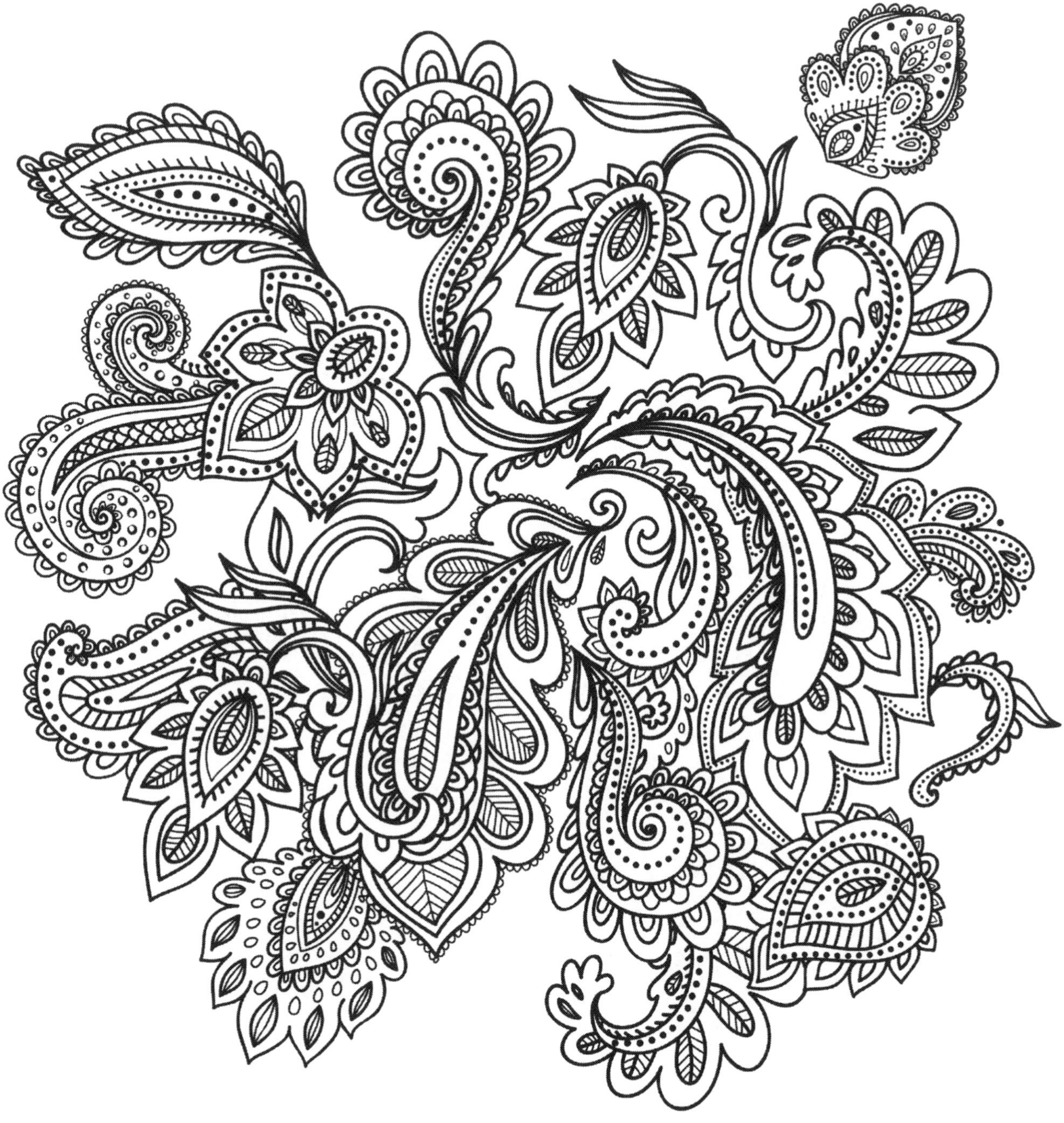

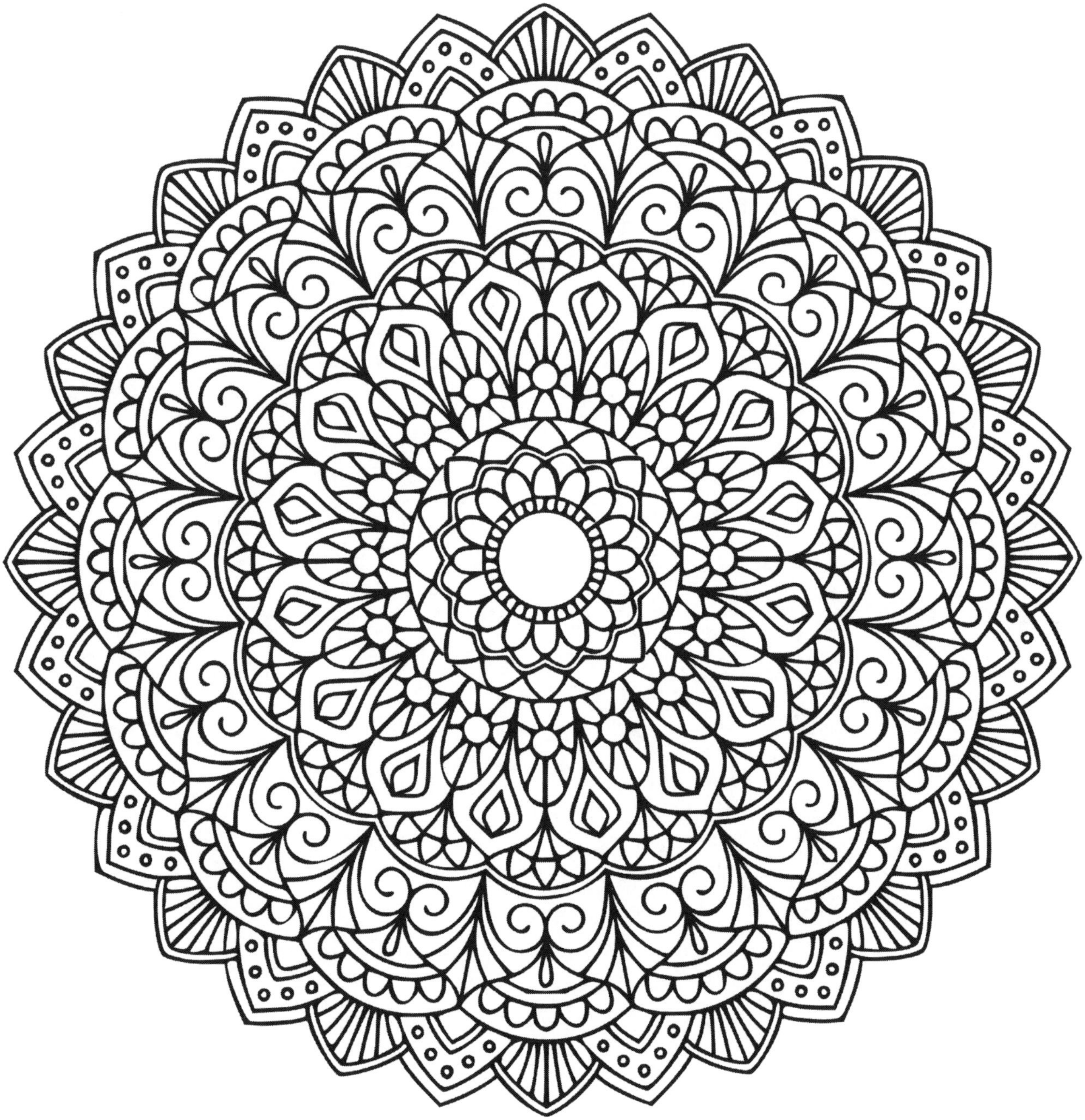

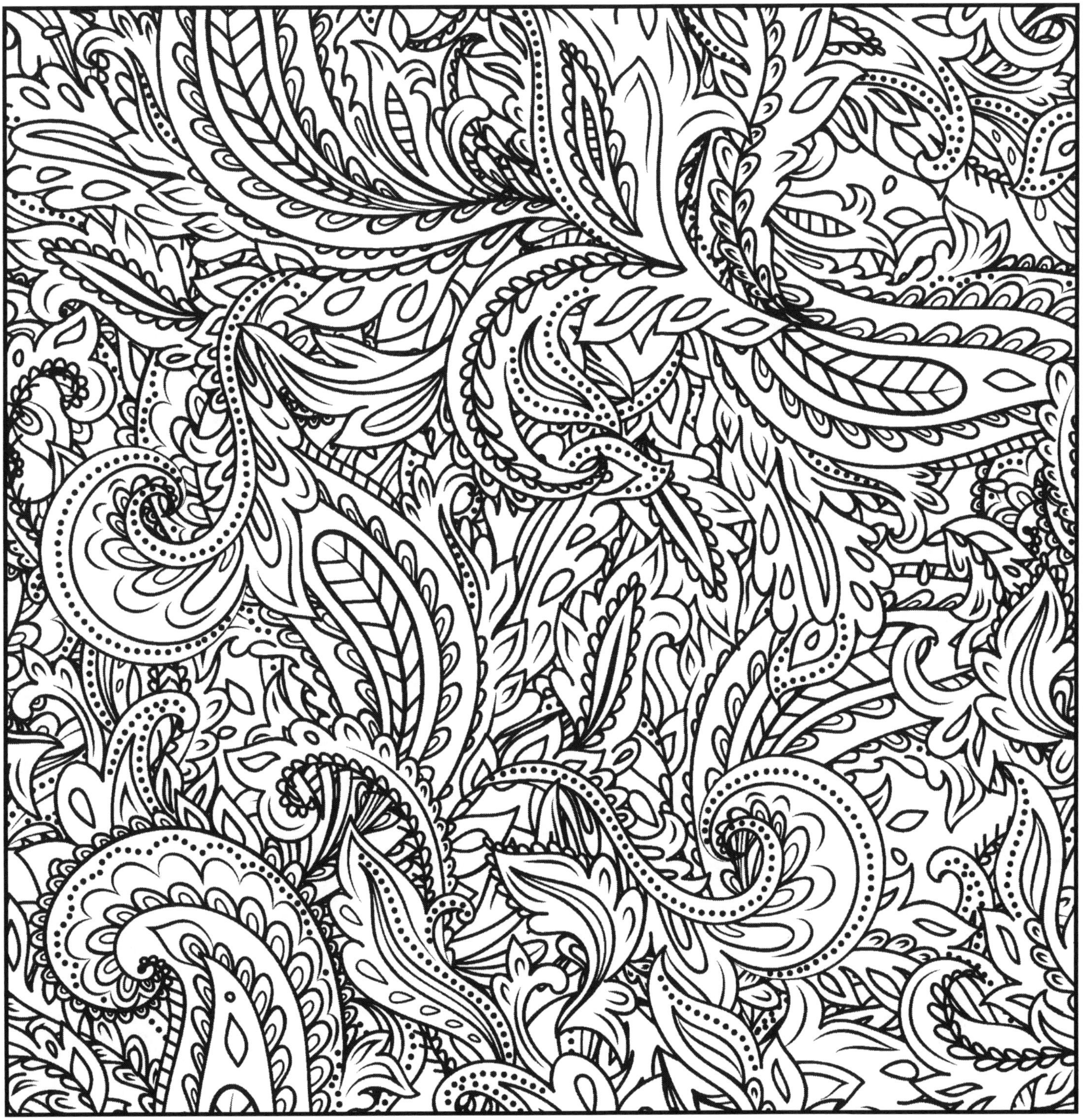

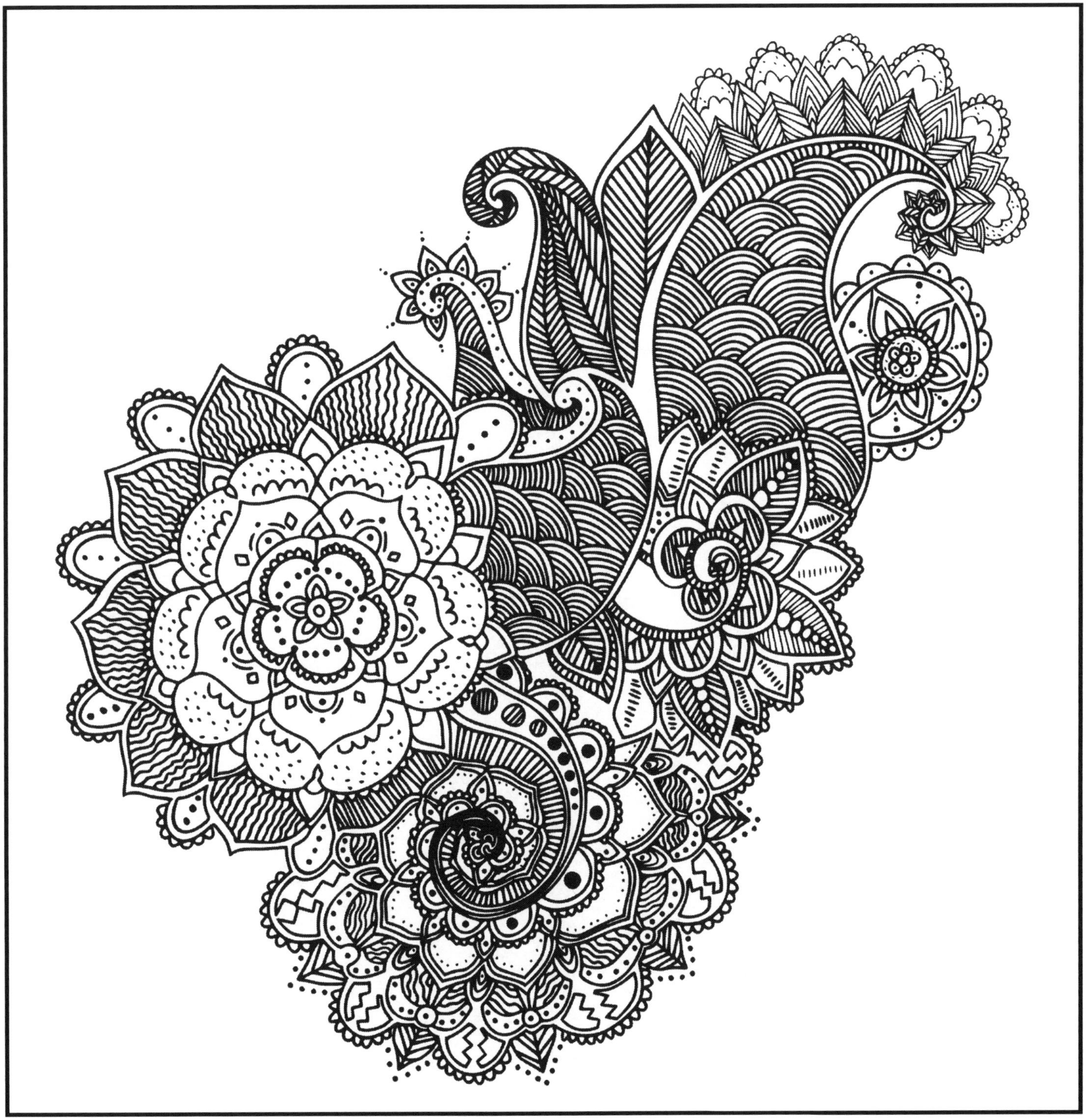

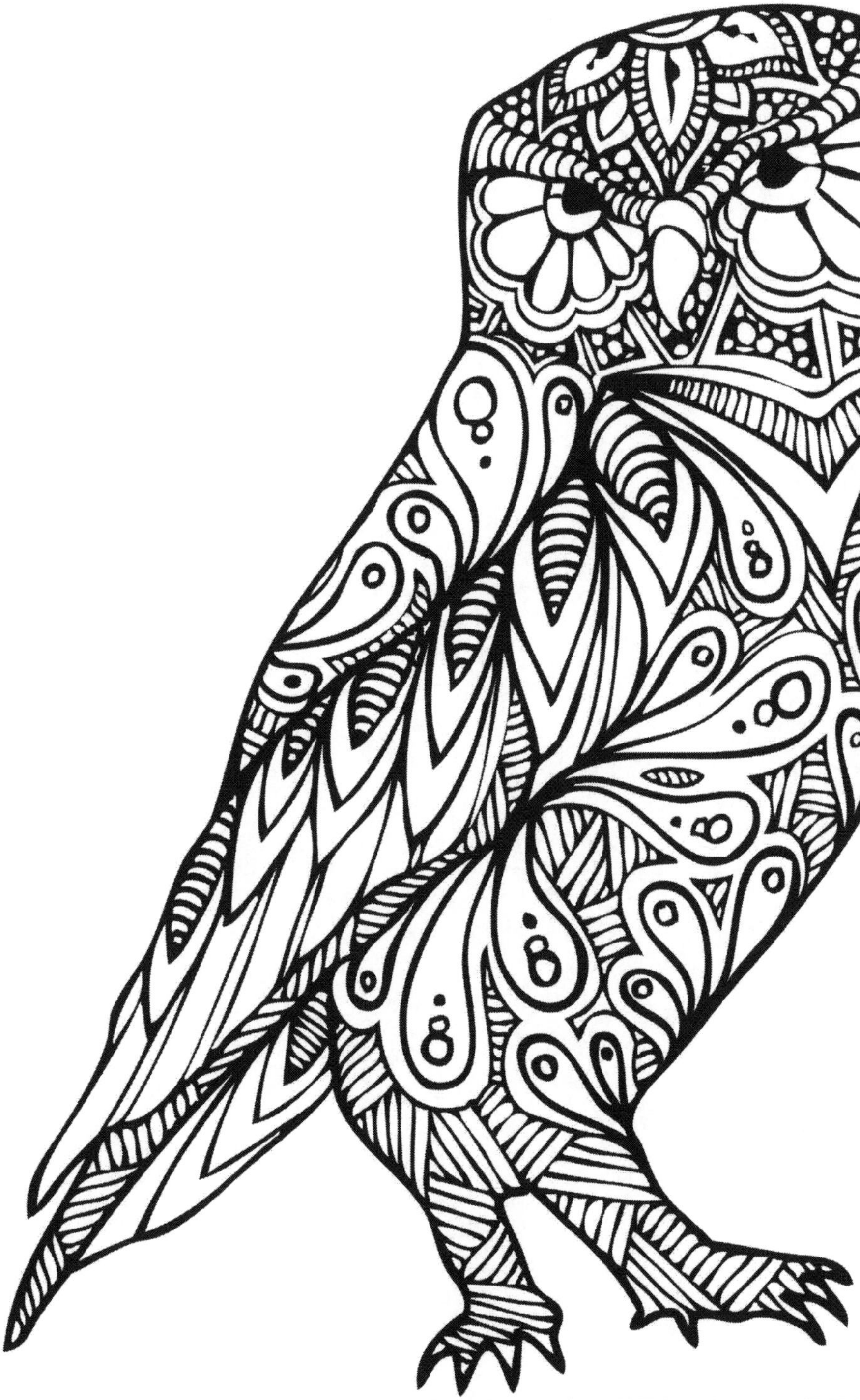

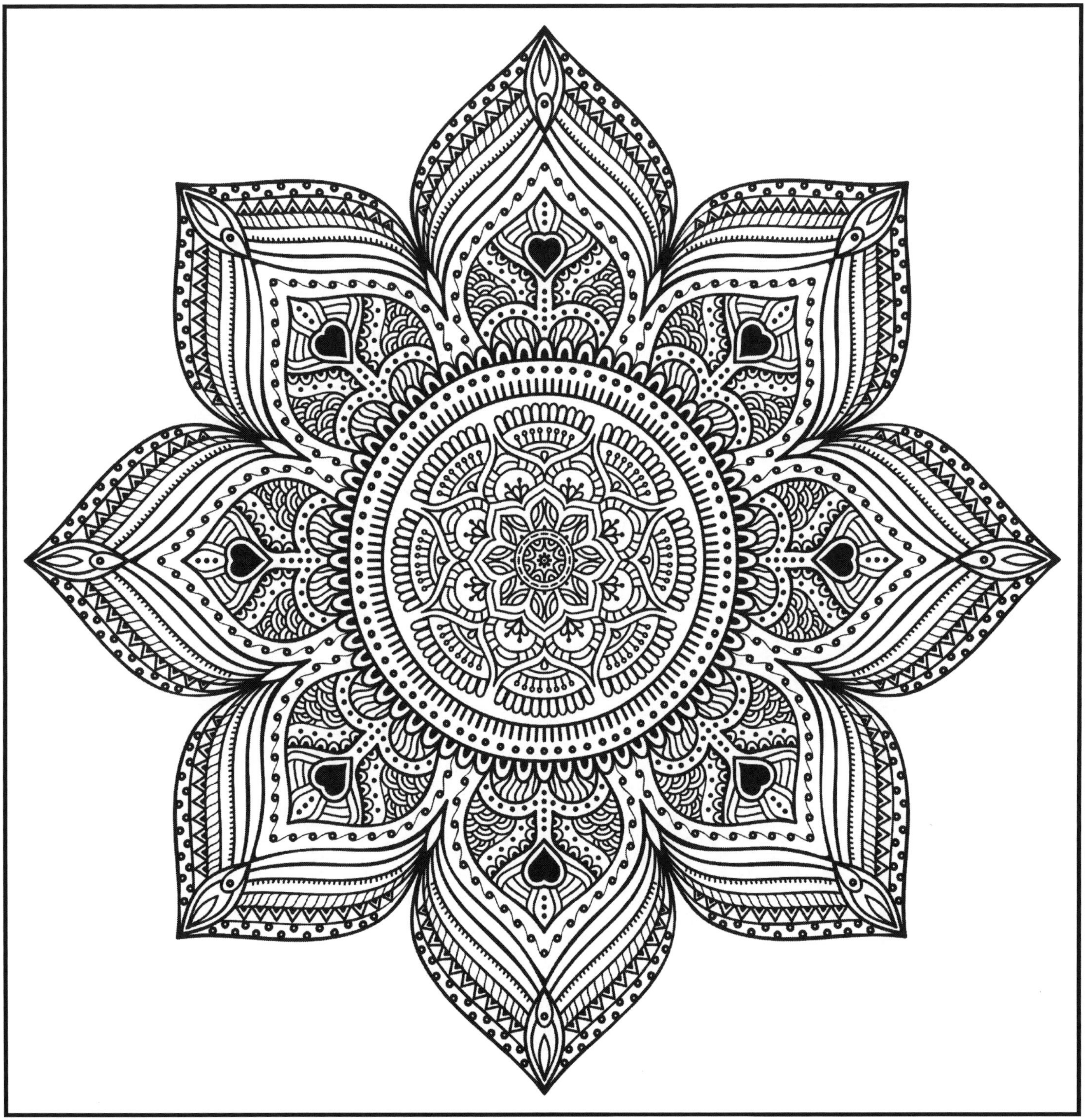

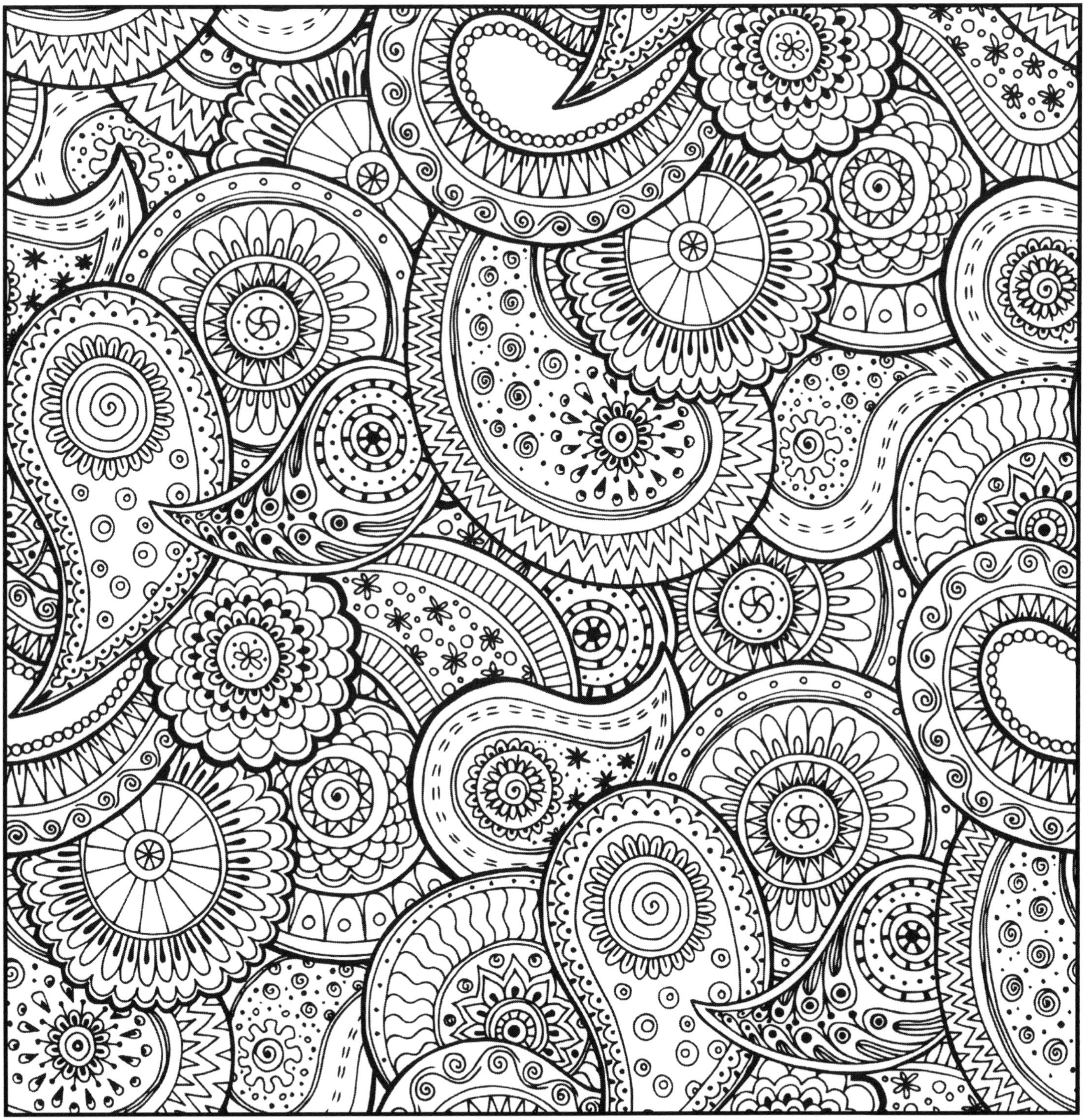

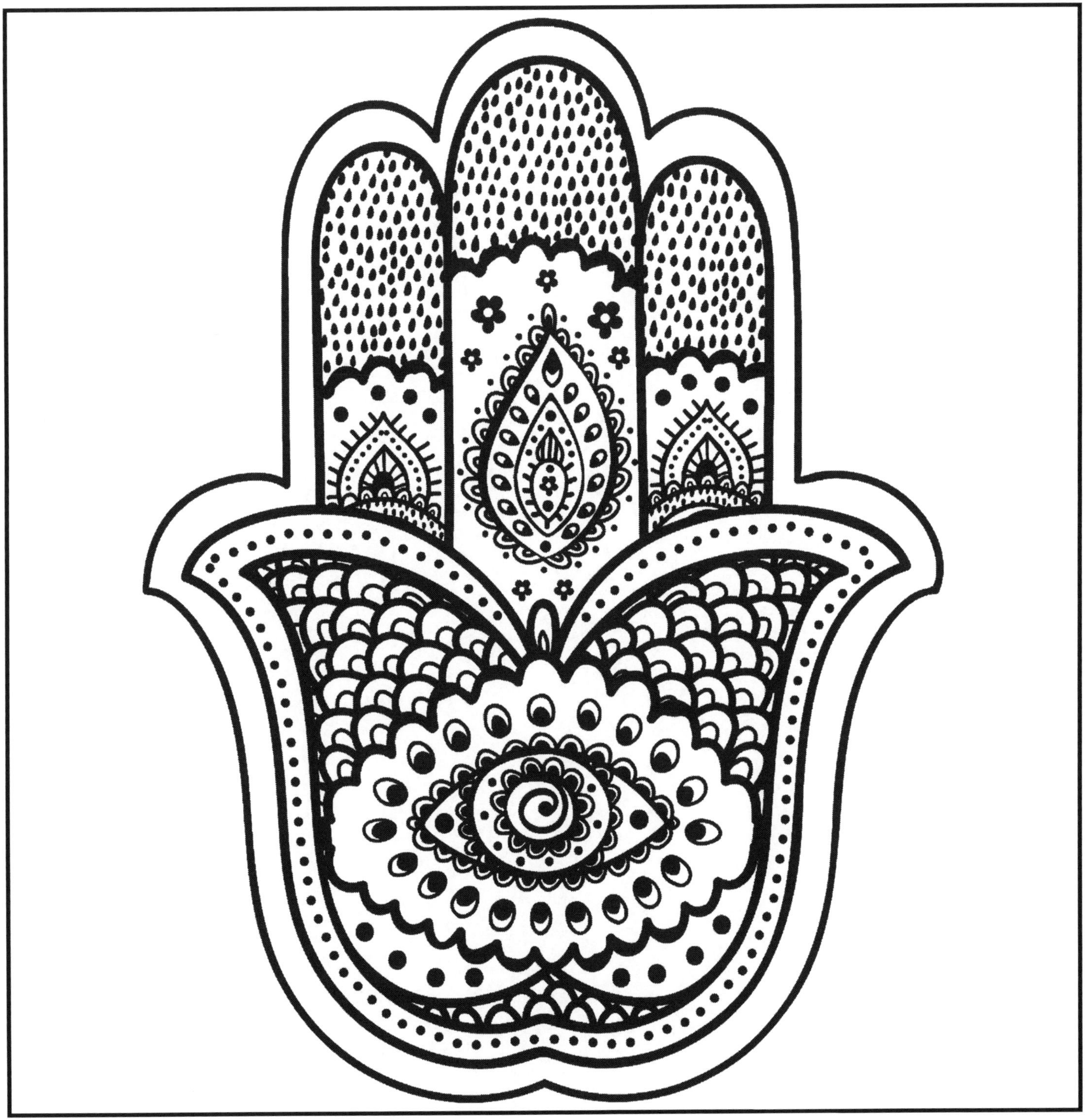

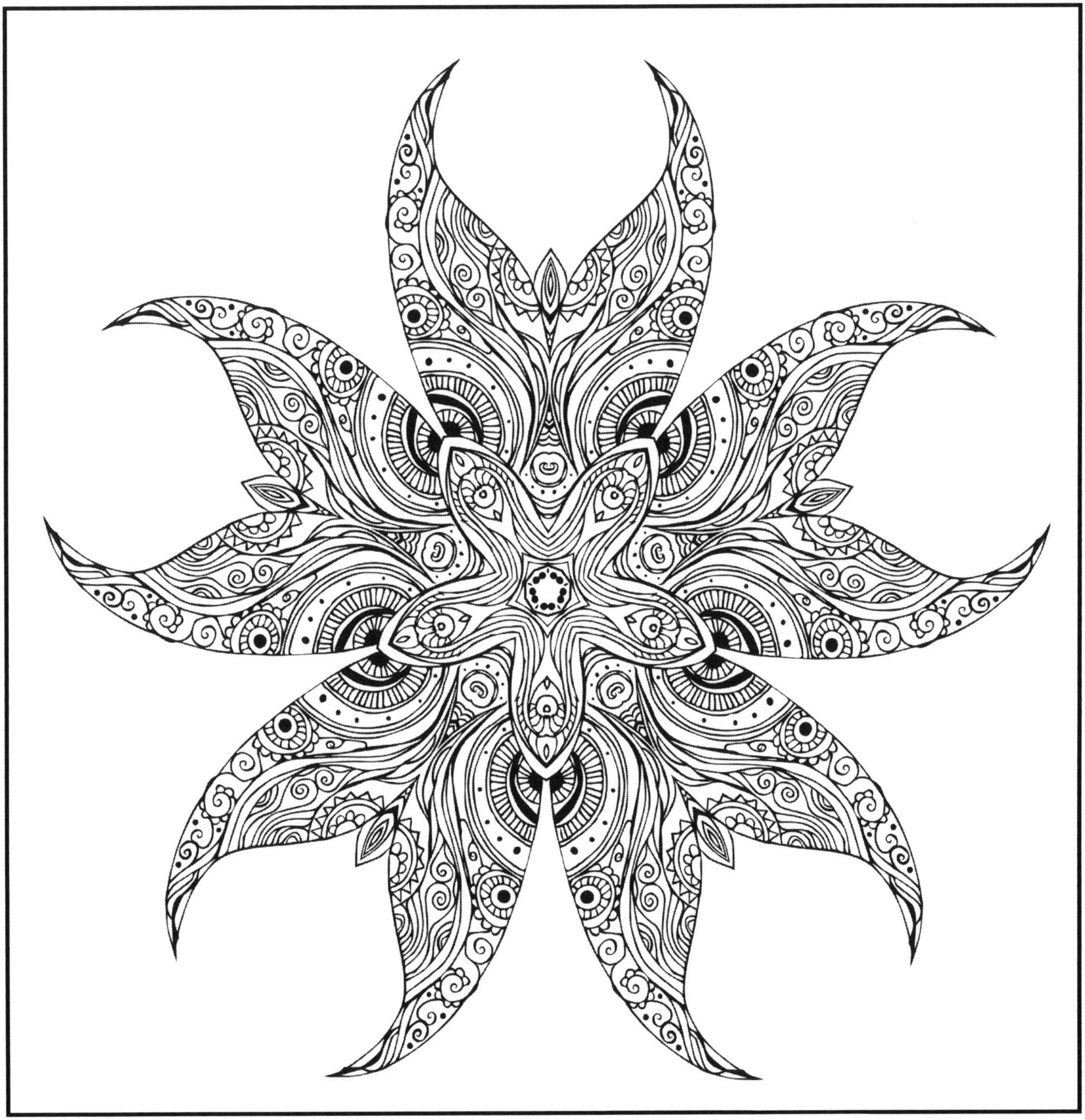

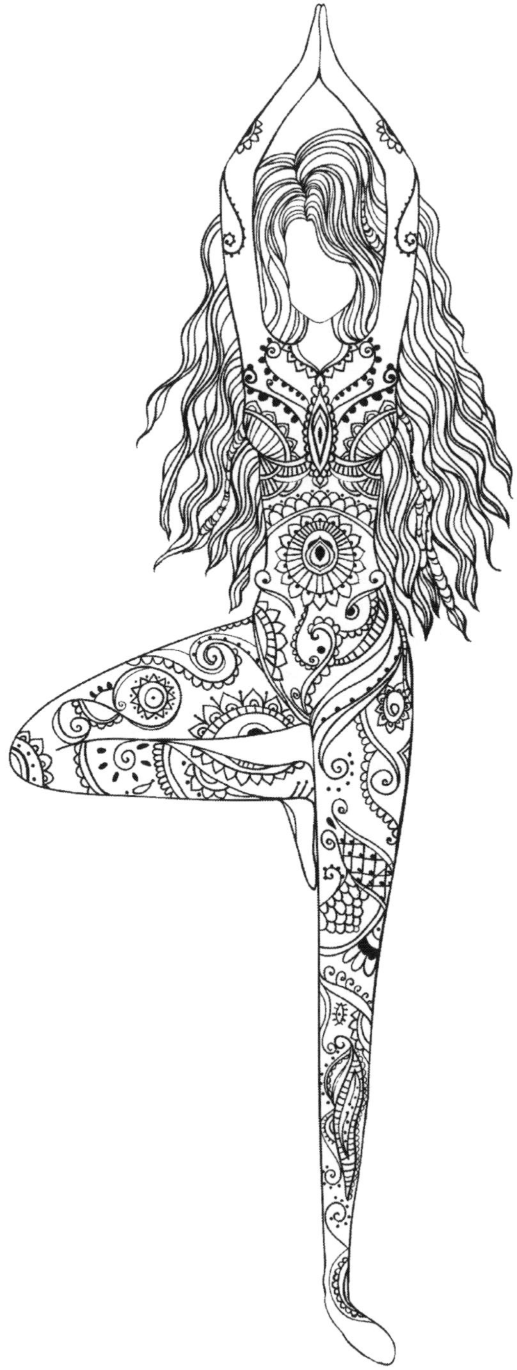

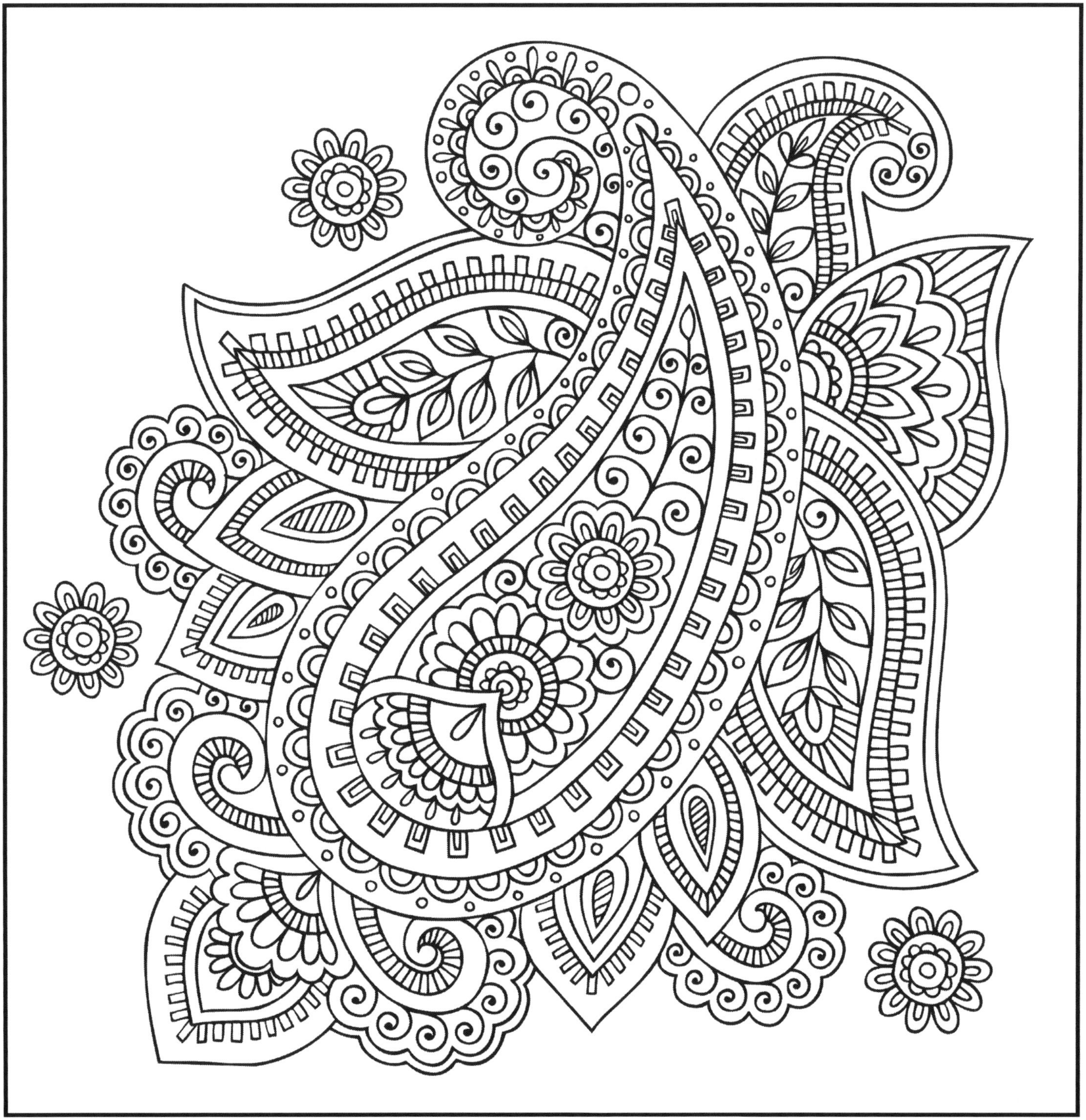

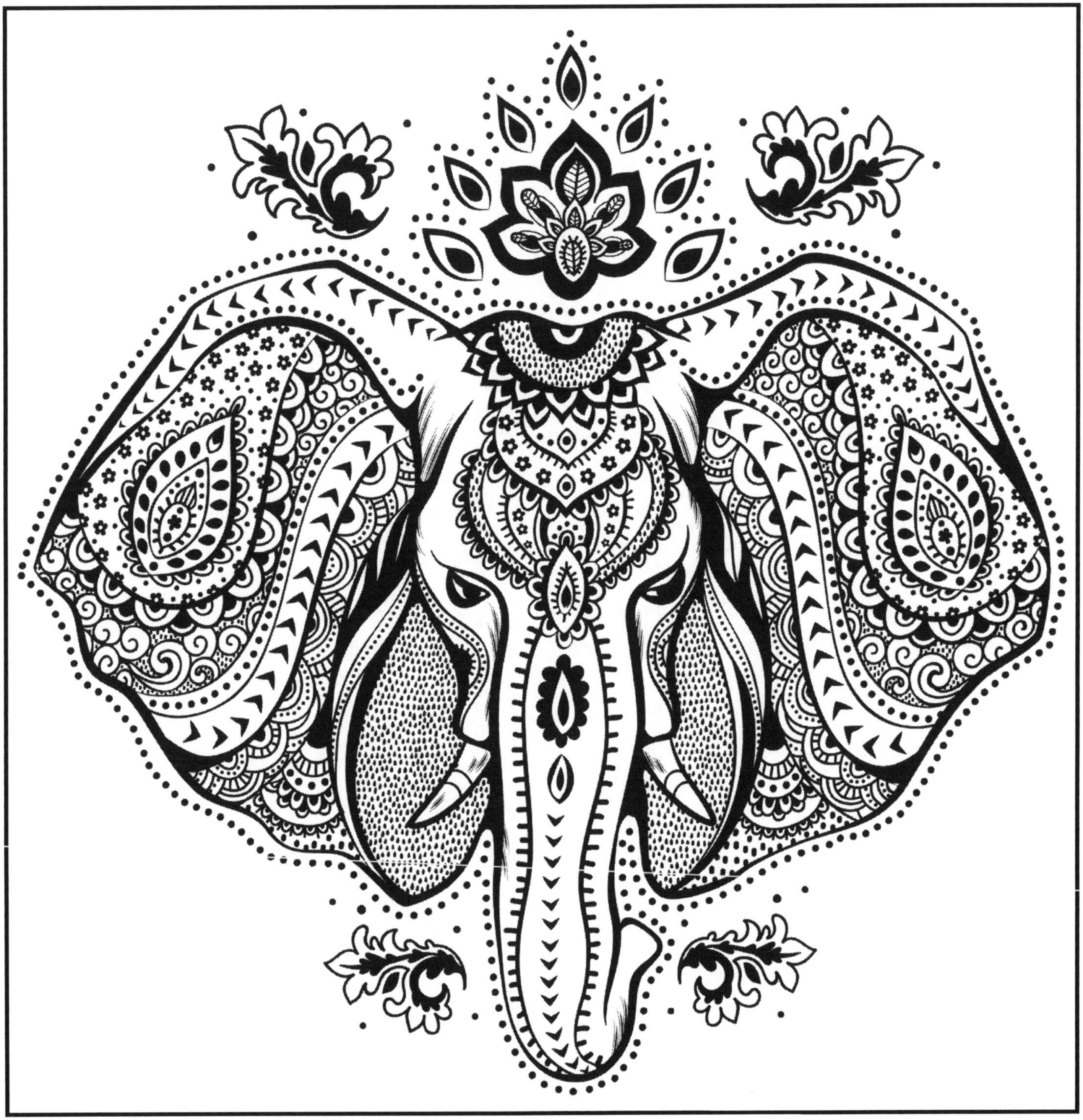

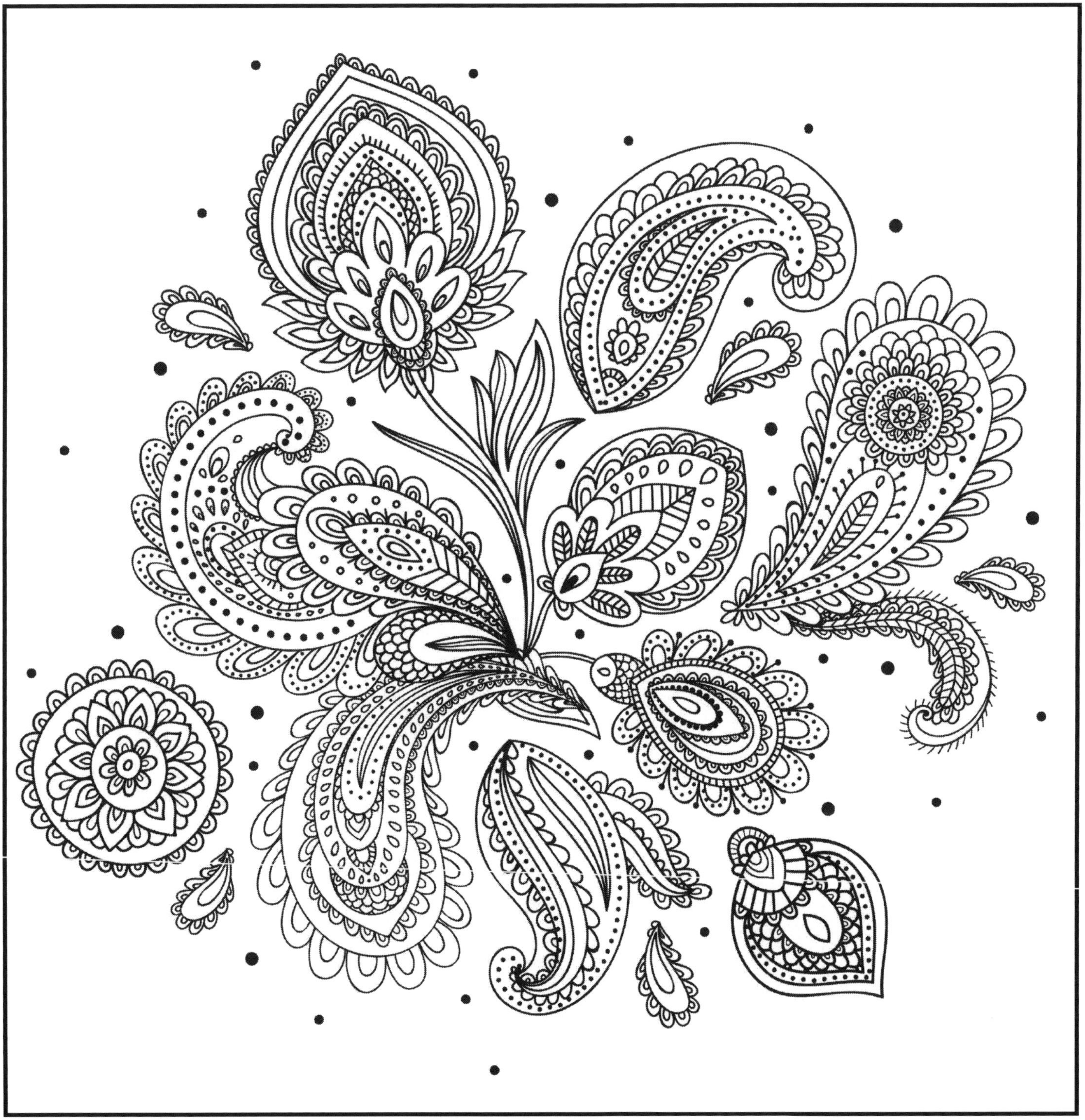

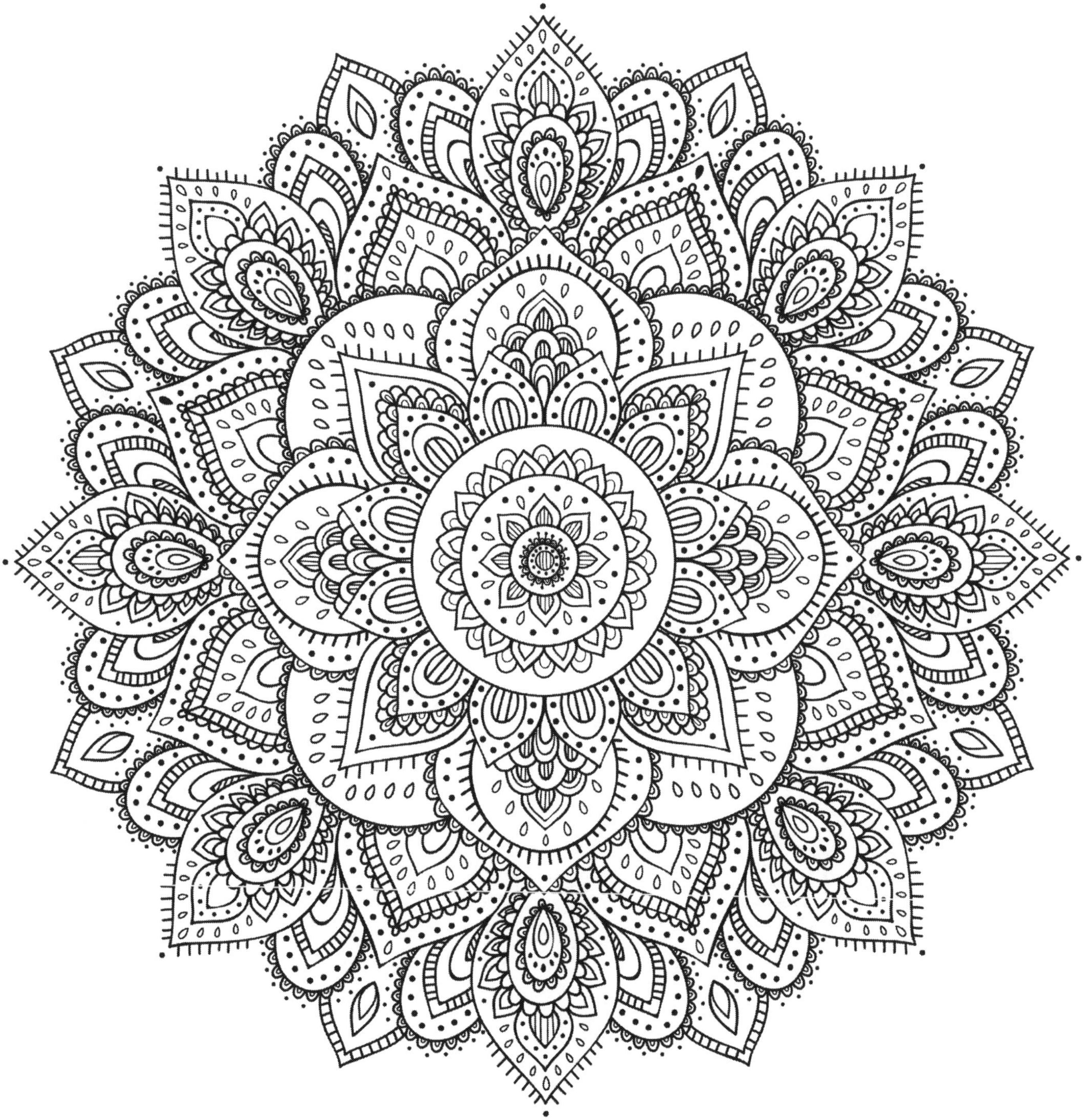

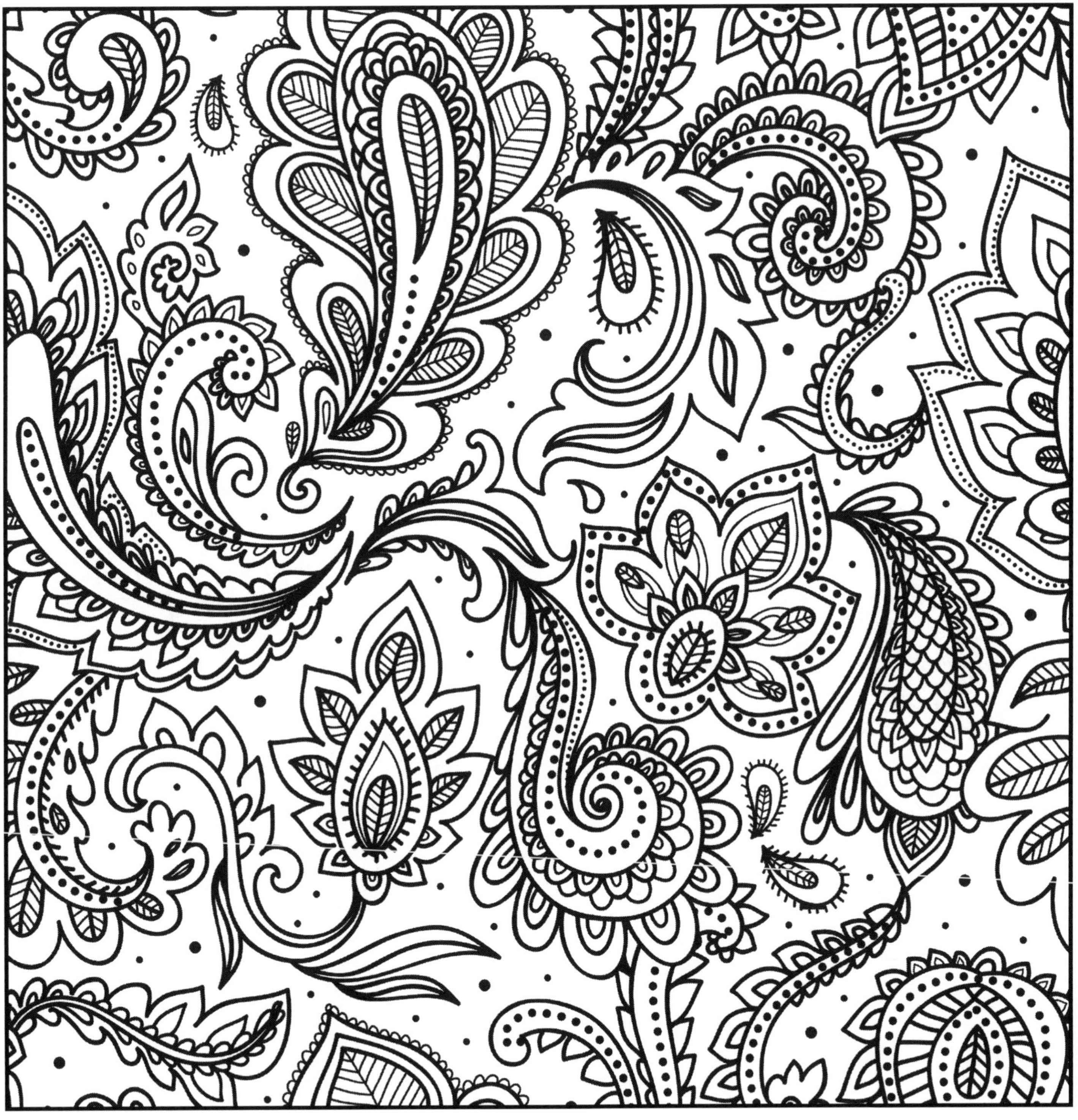

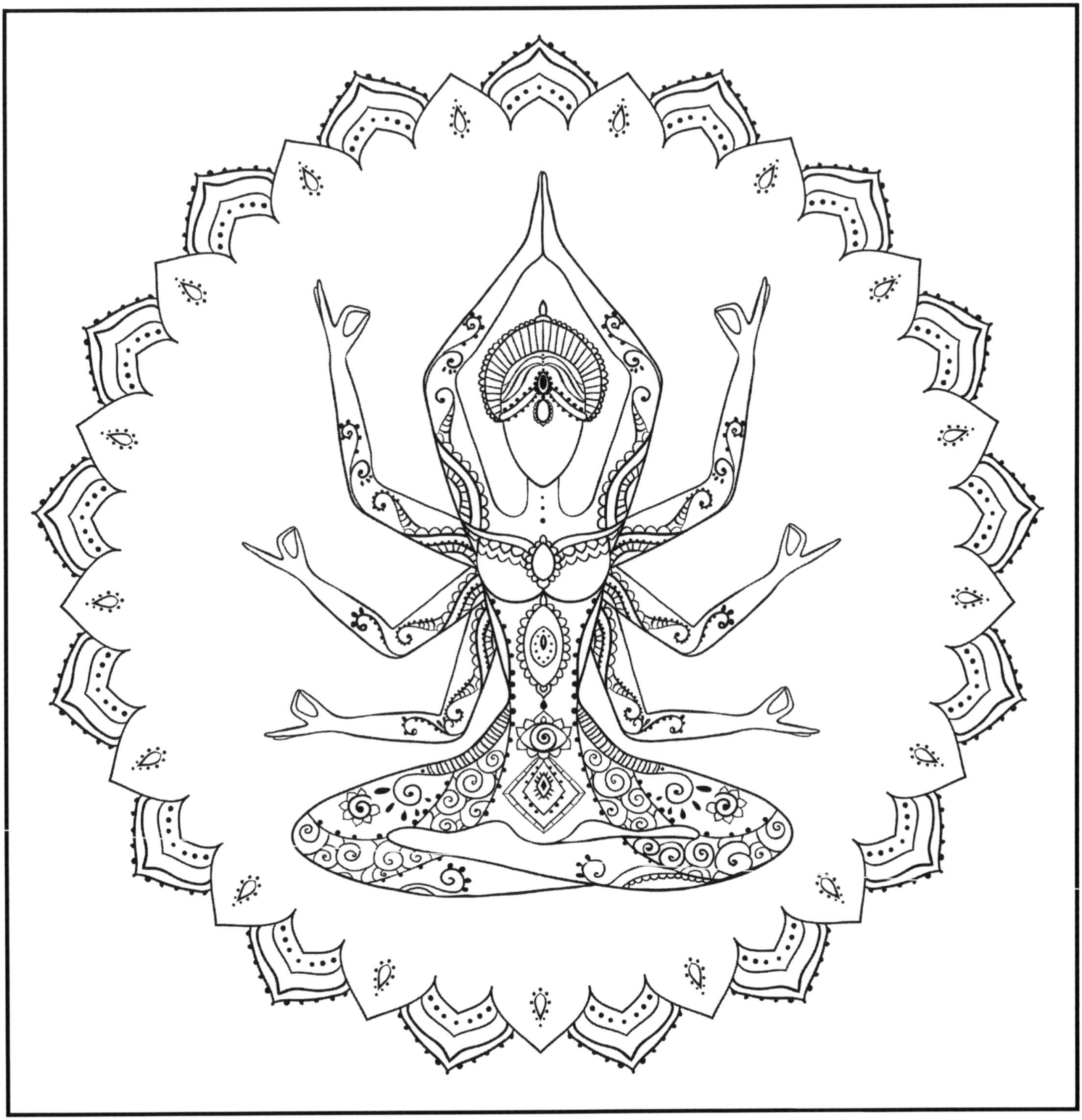

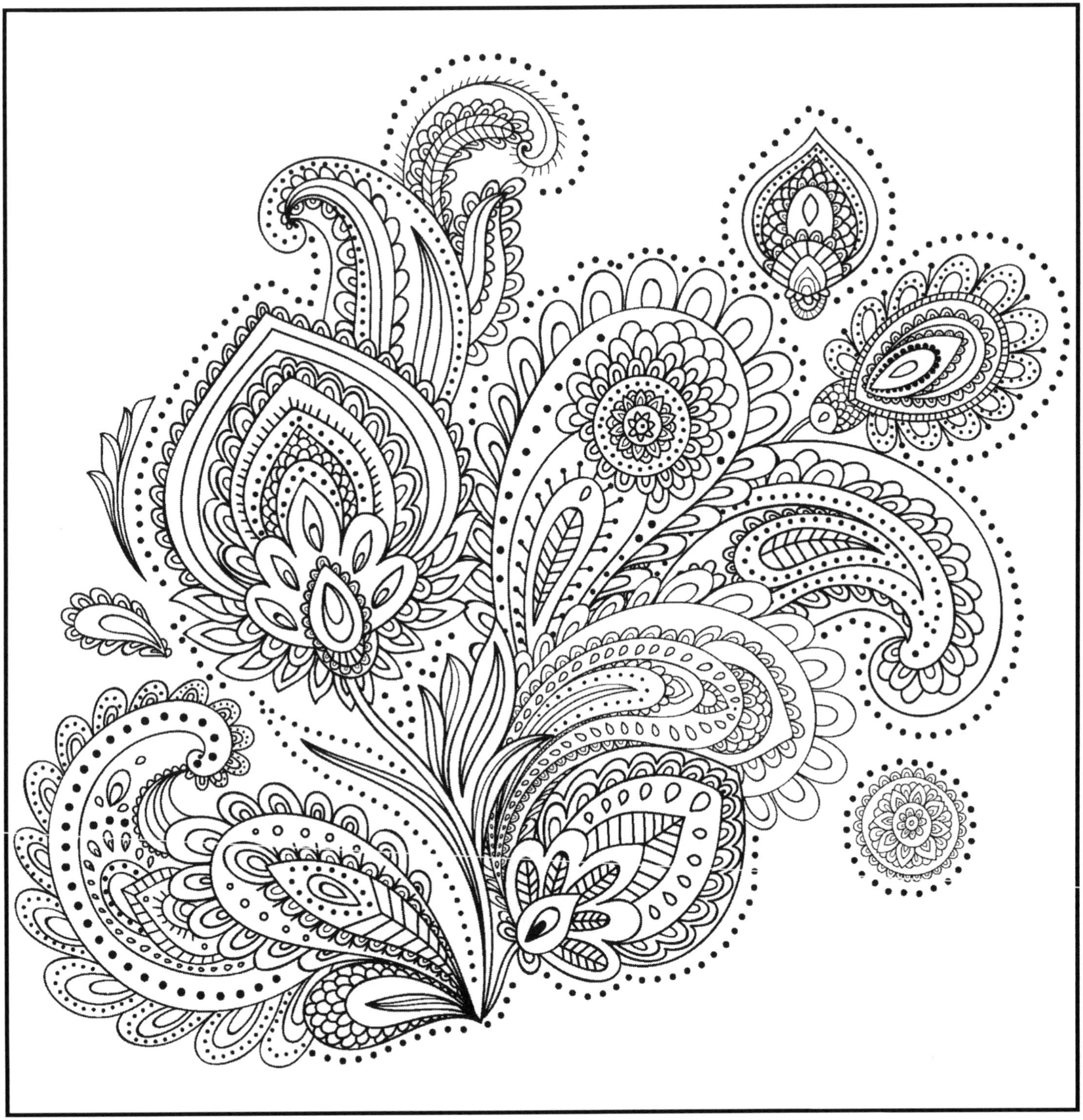

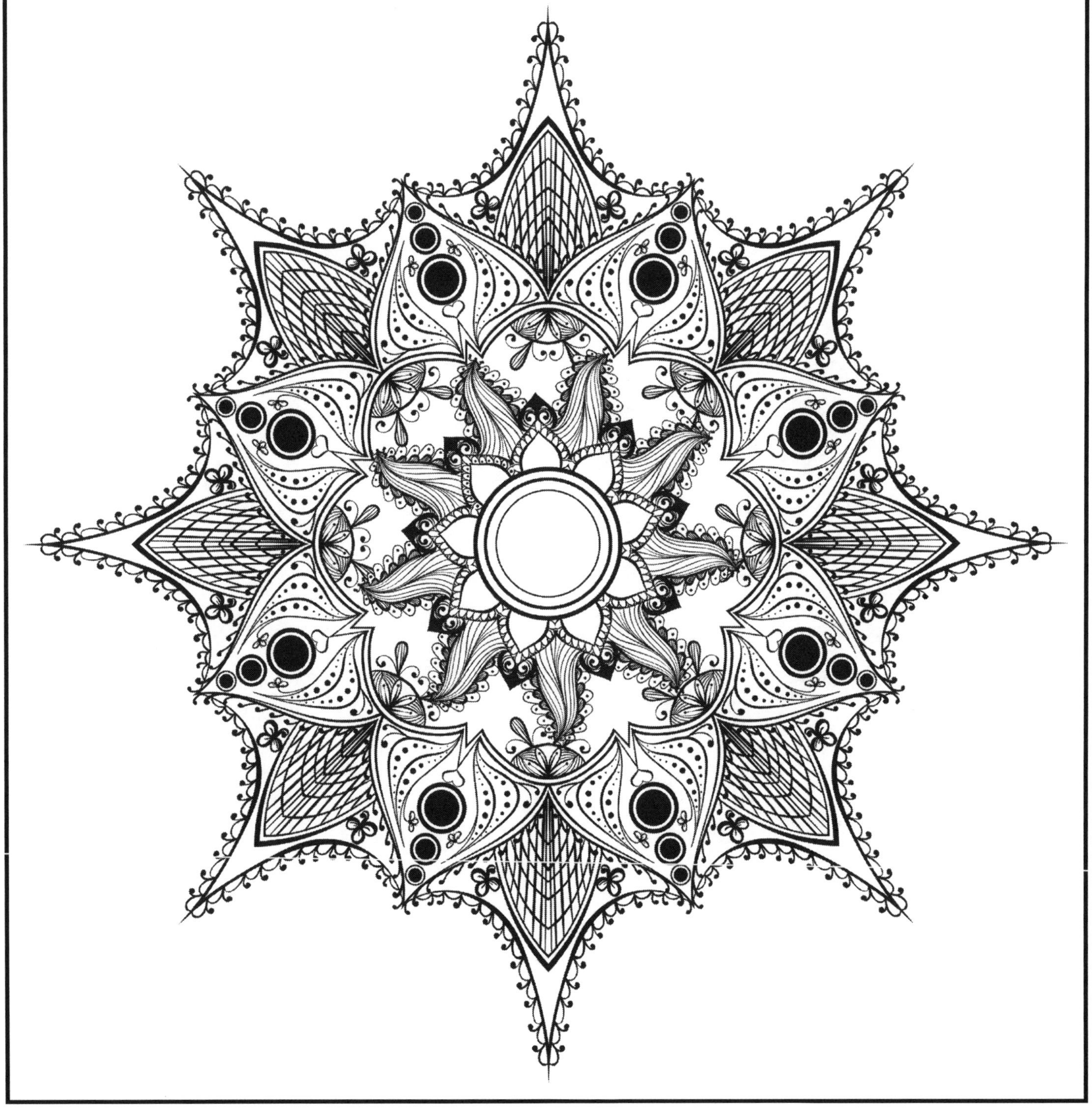

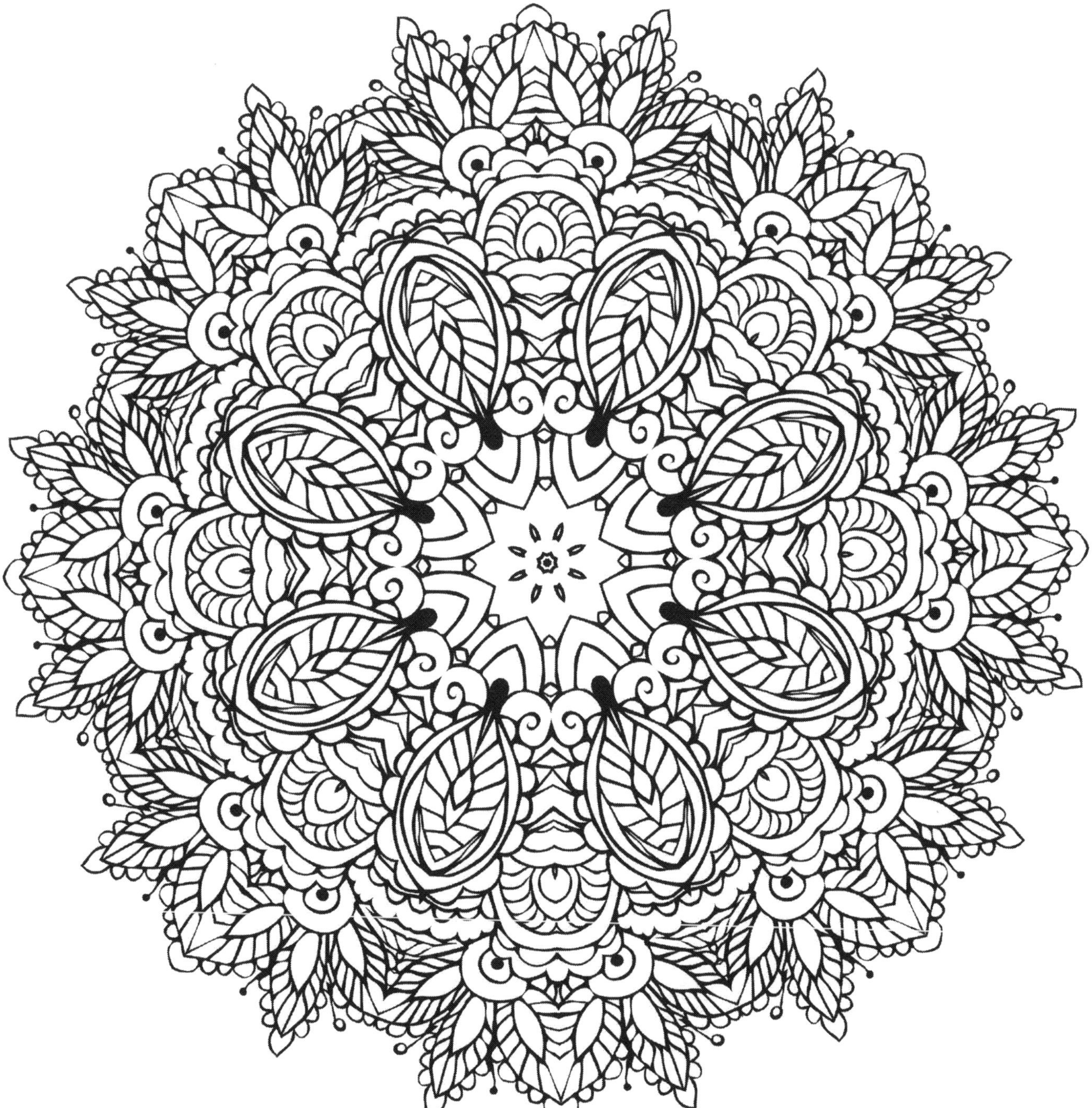

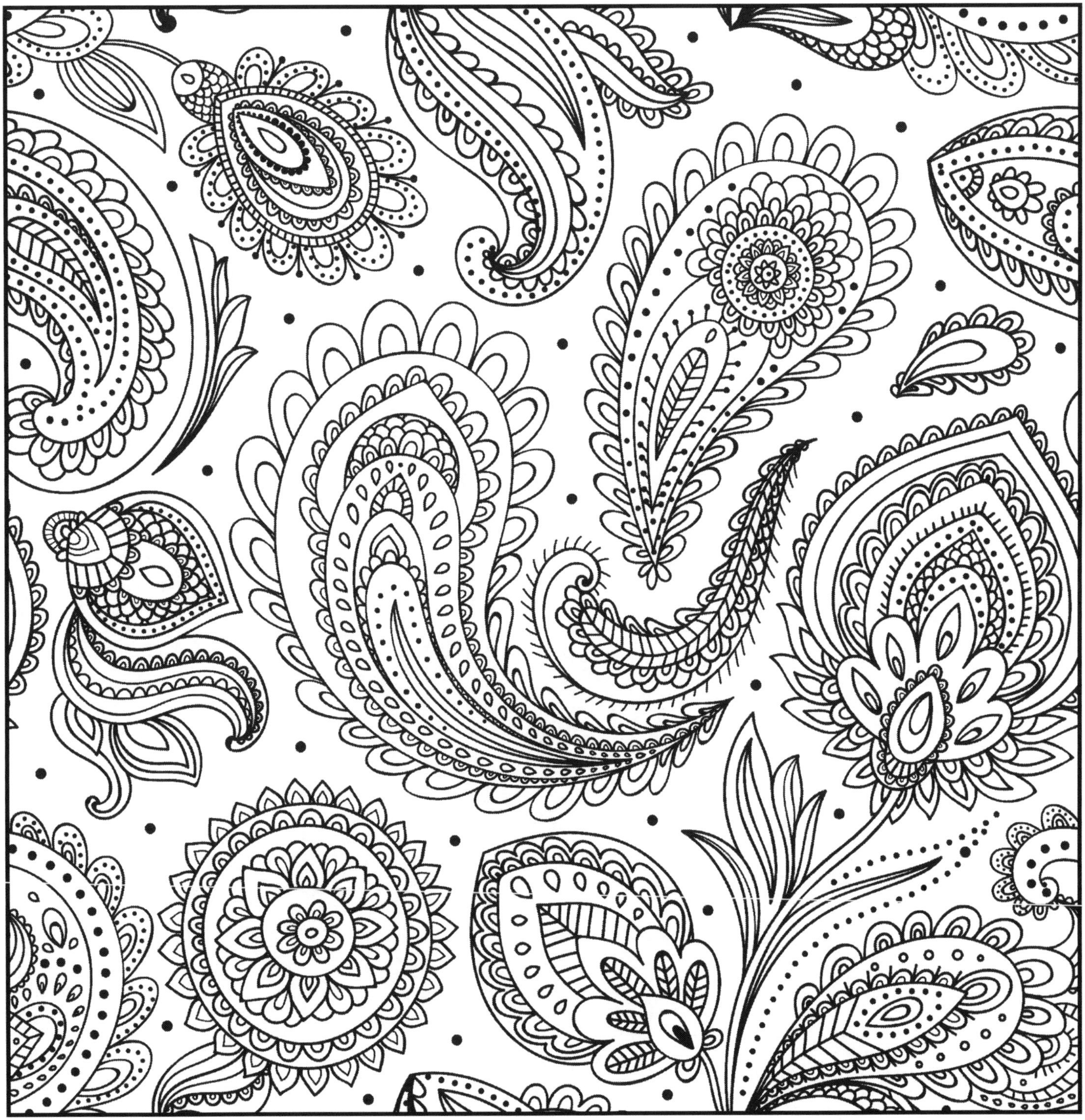

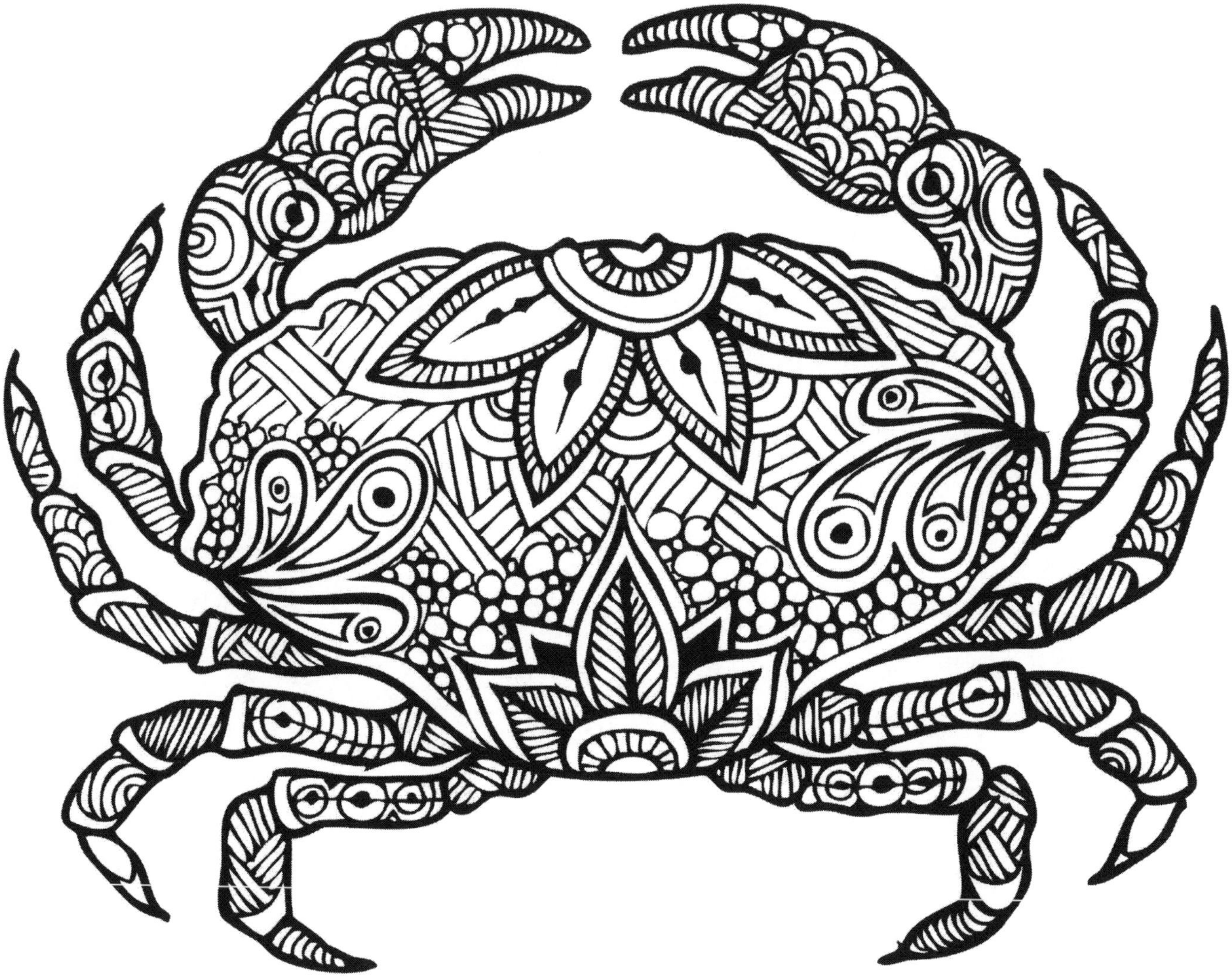

30631926R00057

Made in the USA
San Bernardino, CA
19 February 2016